MORTALISM

BD
431
M86
2003

MORTALISM

Readings on the Meaning of Life

Marcus Aurelius	Lucretius
William Shakespeare	Bede the Venerable
Søren Kierkegaard	Friedrich Nietzsche
Virginia Woolf	Emily Dickinson
David Hume	and more...

Edited by

PETER HEINEGG

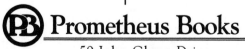

Prometheus Books

59 John Glenn Drive
Amherst, New York 14228-2197

Published 2003 by Prometheus Books

Mortalism: Readings on the Meaning of Life. Copyright © 2003 by Peter Heinegg. All rights reserved. No part of this publication may be reproduced, stored in a retrieval system, or transmitted in any form or by any means, digital, electronic, mechanical, photocopying, recording, or otherwise, or conveyed via the Internet or a Web site without prior written permission of the publisher, except in the case of brief quotations embodied in critical articles and reviews.

Inquiries should be addressed to
Prometheus Books, 59 John Glenn Drive, Amherst, New York 14228–2197
VOICE: 716–691–0133, ext. 207; FAX: 716–564–2711
WWW.PROMETHEUSBOOKS.COM

07 06 05 04 03   5 4 3 2 1

Library of Congress Cataloging-in-Publication Data

Mortalism : readings on the meaning of life / edited by Peter Heinegg.
      p. cm.
   Includes bibliographical references.
   ISBN 1–59102–042–5 (pbk. : alk. paper)
   1. Life. 2. Death. I. Heinegg, Peter.

BD431.M886 2003
128'.5—dc21
                                                                         2003041394

Printed in the United States of America on acid-free paper

To the memory of my mother,

Arlene Willis Heinegg,
1921–1997

CONTENTS

7

INTRODUCTION

The first time I typed the word "mortalism" into my computer, the spell check flagged it in red; and, in its best idiot-savant manner, it still does. Many dictionaries have no entry for the word. This is strange, since the belief that the soul—or spark of life, or animating principle, or whatever—dies with the body is one of the most logical and credible ideas ever to have dawned on the human race, and quite possibly—at least as far as Western civilization goes—has never been more widespread than now.

Apart from being the personal credo of many of the greatest philosophers, mortalism has been the burden of vast portions of Western literature, especially poetry, from Homer to the present—not to mention almost the entire Old Testament.

What follows, then, is a sampling of this mighty but often ignored tradition, a collection of fifty-odd, mostly quite short pieces of poetry and prose that seek to prove, describe, or deal with the obvious (isn't it?) fact that, whatever the meaning of human life, death is its irrevocable end.

Of course, such a belief might very well lead to further negative conclusions, to angst, despair, absurdity, pessimism, and so on; and readers will find some of that here. But the main focus will be on the painful (but perhaps also relieving) truth that is not only proclaimed by the "godless," but is acknowledged even more tellingly, if accidentally, by some of the most earnest believers in an afterlife: that, as Paul said in 1 Corinthians 15.32, "If the dead are not raised, 'Let us eat and drink, for tomorrow we die.' " The most celebrated modern example of this is Tennyson, whose *In Memoriam* has Nature sternly declare:

> A thousand types [species] are gone,
> I care for nothing, all shall go.
> Thou makest thine appeal to me:
> I bring to life, I bring to death:
> The spirit does but mean the breath:
> I know no more.

(56, 3–8)

For the last two millennia at least, tightrope-walking theists have been keenly aware that, should the safety net of resurrection fail, there is nothing between them and the solid ground of mortalism.

The notion of inevitable and permanent extinction is widely associated with Epicurus (d. 270 B.C.E.); that Greek sage, better known by his many illustrious disciples than by his own works, most of which have been lost, is the hero of this book. "In Christian times," writes David John Furley, "Epicureanism was anathema because it taught that man is mortal, that the cosmos is the result of accident, that there is no providential god, and that the criterion of the good life is pleasure."[1] Heretical theses all, in theistic circles, then and now, but also unexceptionable tenets of modern secularism; and readers may be surprised at the large numbers and incredible distinction of the singers in the chorus of mortalism that follows.

NOTE

1. *The Oxford Companion to Classical Civilization* (New York: Oxford University Press, 1998), p. 261.

WHY I AM A MORTALIST

*An odd thought strikes me—we shall
shall receive no letters in the grave.*

—Samuel Johnson

Everybody knows that the soul dies with the body, but nobody likes to admit it. *Moi non plus.* Having been raised a Catholic, I was taught to believe in the "resurrection of the body and the life of the world to come." (To the Church's credit, it never tried to populate eternity with disembodied immortal souls; it opted instead for "glorified bodies," though they would have to wait till Judgment Day to rejoin their owners.) But believing and imagining are two different things. It was and is impossible to conceive of an afterlife except as an improved version of this life (harps, houris, etc.), which doesn't get one very far.

Most Catholics (and other Christians, I assume) take a fideistic leap in the dark on this one. As a teenager, I especially resonated to Gerard Manley Hopkins' tortured cry in "That Nature is a Heraclitean Fire and of the Comfort of the Resurrection":

Man, how fast his firedint, I his mark on mind, is gone!
Both are in an unfathomable, all is in an enormous dark

11

Drowned. O pity and indig | nation! Manshape, that shone
Sheer off, disseveral, a star, | death blots black out; nor
                        mark
Is any of him at all so stark
But vastness blurs and time | beats level. Enough! the
                        Resurrection,
A heart's-clarion! Away grief's gasping, | joyless days,
                        dejection.
     Across my foundering deck shone
A beacon, an eternal beam. | Flesh fade, and mortal trash
Fall to the residuary worm; | world's wildfire, leave but ash:
     In a flash, at a trumpet crash,
I am all at once what Christ is, | since he was what I am, and
This Jack, joke, poor potsherd, | patch, matchwood, immortal
    diamond,
     Is immortal diamond.

Well, that had a joyous ring to it, but in his desperation the poet had been driven to grasping not at straws but at minerals—the only usable metaphor we have for endless duration.

Any more tangible visions of life after death inevitably had something ridiculous about them, whether splendid-silly Baroque Assumptions of the Virgin, with saints and angels floating off with Mary into a trompe-l'oeil, cumulus-filled firmament, or the preposterous Mormon film I saw once in Salt Lake City, which showed families (tall, blond, dressed in bedsheets) of Latter-Day Saints joyously welcoming one another in the Great Beyond. (Let's see, what's the first thing you'd say, after a hug and a high-five? "Made it!" or "Is everybody here?" or "How about those Mets!") Such images did more for the cause of unbelief than an atheist's jibes.

Anyhow, in my twenties and thirties the case for mortalism grew stronger. I read the mortalists: Epicurus, Lucretius (the supreme master), Montaigne (a member of the club despite his pro forma Christianity), Rochester, Hume, Diderot, Heine, and from then on practically every serious modern writer, apart from a few rearguard protestors like Dostoyevsky or T. S. Eliot. More importantly I felt periodic gusts of wind blowing in from the "vast deserts of eternity." One such blast (there were many more) came in July, 1971 when I was flying at night into Tehran from Ankara. Approaching an alien, forbidding metropolis (who knew Farsi?), its millions of lights twinkling coldly up at me, I thought of Pascal (a closet mortalist): *combien de royaumes nous ignorent!* "How many kingdoms have no idea we exist!" That is to say, our minds, our selves were tiny, evanescent flickers in the gigantic void of the cosmos, brief campfires in the dark. Nothing could be easier than to picture them going out. *Le silence éternel de ces espaces infinis m'effraie.* As well it might.

We hug the shore of the familiar world (almost all the universe is a very deep ocean); we try to *make* everything familiar by naming it and qualifying it. In some ways, of course, we succeed; through its "intentional union" with things, our mind has a carnal/cerebral knowledge of the world. But the knower is mortal, and knows it, even if all our perception, as Coleridge said, is a quasi-divine creation (but then, countered Father Freud, we are only prosthetic gods).

None of this qualifies as a great discovery—it was no discovery whatsoever, just an acknowledgment. But the crucial moment or phase finally came when I *felt* it all. No doubt part of a typical midlife crisis, this feeling seems to have been triggered by two events in 1997 (when I was 55): the death of my mother from a stroke, and a one-week (my very first) hospitalization with a pulmonary embolism. At the time I was too caught up in immediate sensations, or the zonked-out absence of them, to figure out what was happening to me. But afterward I found that a continuous, buzzing awareness of facticity, transiency, and mortality had settled into my head.

It was something like Sartrean nausea: a permanent feeling of anxiety and pointlessness. Actually, it was more positive than that, not so much a malaise as an overwhelming realization, akin to the "wonderful concentrating" of the mind that Dr. Johnson (another Christian closet mortalist) ascribes to a man about to be hanged. Colors became bolder, outlines sharper, clear skies more exhilarating, cloudy ones more depressing. I sensed my heart beating, my nerves pulsing, my lungs pumping, my skin tingling from sun and wind, the earth spinning, time passing. Whoosh. I could see and understand myself and others more vividly than before. In a word, I felt mortal.

This is a condition beyond arguments. Metaphysicians and priests (I used to be something of both) may preach or prate about immortality, but the body knows better. As surely as the body knows pain or delight, the onset of orgasm or vomiting, it knows that it (we) will die and disappear. We have a foretaste of this every time we fall asleep or suffer any diminution of consciousness from drugs, fatigue, sickness, accidents, aging, and so forth. The extrapolation from the fading of awareness to its total extinction is (ha) dead certain. First the light flickers on and off, then comes the blackout. No transmigration, transformation, shedding the corporeal husk: just a permanent power outage. My body was/is telling me the truth about itself and the world (repeating, among other things, the old saw: *tout passe, tout lasse, tout casse*). It knows it came from the abyss and is headed there: the most banal—and darkly thrilling—fact imaginable.

But who wants to hear that message? Not me, certainly. Life in general has no use for death; fanatically, programatically self-involved, life is forever busy, fussy, fretting over the future. It's a command and control center that will admit, if pressed, that it could and ultimately will be "knocked out," but in the meantime it goes restlessly on. Many people seem to have instinctively accepted Epicurus' paradox that death means nothing to us, because before our death arrives, it doesn't exist, and once it does, *we* don't exist. For years I lived that way, and

I regret that I can't anymore. For one thing, Epicurus' neat dichotomy ignores the fact that death usually comes by slow, observable degrees, and that we die vicariously every time we scan the obituary page or attend a funeral.

In any event, as far as I'm concerned, mortalism has conquered, has crushed all the alternatives. I don't see that this does me, or anyone else, a great deal of good. (It might, in theory, make one more patient or sympathetic.) But there's no point—or not much—in discussing tastes. In *The Wreck of the Deutschland*, my old idol, Father Hopkins, gives a vivid description of biting into a piece of fruit:

> How a lush-kept plush-capped sloe
> Will, mouthed to flesh—burst,
> Gush!—flush the man, the being with it, sour or sweet
> Brim, in a flash, full!

Exactly. Though a long drench rather than a quick dip, this *is* a taste in my mouth, flooding my lips, tongue, and palate, sour, strong, and utterly irrefutable: death.

So much for the bad news. The good news was that I finally found a permanent label for myself: once a "lapsed" or "fallen-away" Catholic (a quaint pre–Vatican II term, like "living in sin"), I now embraced the Yiddish *apikoyres* (or Hebrew *apikoros*), meaning "a follower of Epicurus," and hence a heretic, a mortalist, and a general unbeliever. I felt I had a right to be a *Jewish* outcast: I was a quarter-Jew (through my paternal grandfather); I had studied and taught the Bible for forty years; I knew a lot of Yiddish and more than a smattering of Hebrew. Since I would inevitably define myself as a rebel and escapee from the Judeo-Christian tradition, let it be from the oldest and noblest part of that tradition, the part I ultimately loved best—even as the word itself served as a reminder of another tradition that aided and abetted that escape—into the void.

They could put it on my gravestone, along with the lines from the *Inferno* (X.13–15) about the tombs of the Epicureans in the Sixth Circle (reserved for heretics, or the violent against God):

> Suo cimitero da questa parte hanno
> con Epicuro tutti suoi seguaci,
> che l'anima col corpo morta fanno.

> Within this region is the cemetery
> of Epicurus and his followers,
> all those who say the soul dies with the body.
>
> (trans. Alan Mandelbaum)

And so say I.

THE EPIC OF GILGAMESH (CA. 2000 B.C.E.)

I n this, the oldest story in the world of which there are written remains, an ancient Sumerian tale, passed on by the Assyrians, we hear the first great protest against mortality—and learn that there is no point in fighting it. Gilgamesh, the king of Uruk (a city on the Euphrates in modern-day Iraq), has the impossible genetic makeup of two-thirds divinity and one-third humanity; i.e., he is human enough to die. Once Gilgamesh realizes that, beautiful, strong, and omnicompetent though he is, he is doomed to disappear forever, he makes heroic efforts to get around his destiny. He even manages to find the flower of immortality, but a serpent steals it, and all his efforts come to naught.

GILGAMESH PROTESTS TO SHAMASH, THE SUN GOD

O Shamash, hear me, hear me, Shamash, let my voice be heard. Here in the city man dies oppressed at heart, man perishes with despair in his heart, I have looked over the wall and I see the bodies floating on the river, and that will be my lot also. Indeed I know it is so, for whoever is tallest among men cannot reach the heavens, and the greatest cannot encompass the earth.

GILGAMESH SPEAKS WITH SIDURI, THE GODDESS OF WINE

Then Siduri said to him, ". . . Why are your cheeks so starved and is your face so drawn? Why is despair in your heart and your face like the face of one who has made a long journey? Yes, why is your face burned from heat and cold. And why do you come here wandering over the pastures in search of the wind?"

Gilgamesh answered her, "And why should not my cheeks be starved and my face drawn? Despair is in my heart and my face is the face of one who has made a long journey, it was burned with heat and cold. Why should I not wander over the pastures in search of the wind? My friend, my younger brother, he who hunted the wild ass of the wilderness and the panther of the plains, my friend, my younger brother who

15

seized and killed the Bull of Heaven . . . my friend who was very dear to me and who endured dangers beside me, Enkidu my brother, whom I loved, the end of mortality has overtaken him. I wept for him seven days and nights till the worm fastened on him. Because of my brother I am afraid of death, because of my brother I stray through the wilderness and cannot rest. But now, young woman, maker of wine, since I have seen your face do not let me see the face of death which I dread so much."

She answered, "Gilgamesh, where are you hurrying to? You will never find that life for which you are looking. When the gods created man they allotted to him death, but life they retained in their own keeping. As for you, Gilgamesh, fill your belly with good things; day and night, night and day, dance and be merry, feast and rejoice. Let your clothes be fresh, bathe yourself in water, cherish the little child that holds your hand, and make your wife happy in your embrace; for this too is the lot of man." (Cf. Ecclesiastes 9.7–9)

THE DEATH OF GILGAMESH

The destiny was fulfilled which the father of the gods, Enlil of the mountain, had decreed for Gilgamesh: "In nether-earth the darkness will show him a light: of mankind, all that are known, none will leave a monument for generations to come to compare with his. The heroes, the wise men, like the new moon have their waxing and waning. Men will say, 'Who has ever ruled with might and with power like him?' As in the dark month, the month of shadows, so without him there is no light. O Gilgamesh, this was the meaning of your dream. You were given the kingship, such was your destiny, everlasting life was not your destiny'."

The king has laid himself down and will not rise again,
The Lord of Kullah will not rise again;
He overcame evil, he will not come again;
Though he was strong of arm he will not rise again;

He had wisdom and a comely face, he will not come again;
He is gone into the mountain, he will not come again;
On the bed of fate he lies, he will not rise again,
From the couch of many colors he will not come again.

The people of the city, great and small, are not silent; they lift up the lament, all men of flesh and blood lift up the lament. Fate has spoken; like a hooked fish he lies stretched on the bed, like a gazelle that is caught in a noose. Inhuman Namtar [Fate] is heavy upon him, Namtar that has neither hand nor foot, that drinks no water and eats no meat.

(trans. N. K. Sandars)

THE BIBLE

The Hebrew Bible (or Old Testament) might seem like an odd source of material on mortalism, but it's actually a mortalist goldmine. Right from the start—for example, in the death scenes of the patriarchs—many biblical texts make it perfectly clear that personal life is ending forever: "These are the days of Abraham's life, a hundred and seventy-five years. Abraham breathed his last and died in a good old age, an old man and full of years, was gathered to his people" (Gen. 25.7–8). Not until the very latest book in the Hebrew Bible, Daniel (second century B.C.E.) do we find a clear-cut (and very brief) affirmation of life after death. In fact the whole focus of *Tanakh* (the Jewish acronym for the Bible: *T* for Torah, *N* for *Neviim* or "prophets," *Kh* for *Khetuvim* or "writings") is on the here and now, where God rewards and punishes his people and all humans. The so-called Deuteronomic Principle affirms that those who do good will fare well and those who violate God's laws will suffer miserably—in this life.

Of course, the world itself often fails to work this way, and so among the Bible's most powerful passages are from two examples of "wisdom literature," Job and Ecclesiastes, where the speakers reflect mournfully on the finality of death as evidence that there is no justice—or not much—in human life. The texts that follow cannot be dated precisely, but they likely come from some time after the Exile (587–538 B.C.E.)

JOB 11–19

11 "Why did I not die at birth,
   come forth from the womb and expire?

12 Why did the knees receive me?
   Or the breasts, that I should suck?

13 For then I should have lain down and be quiet;
   I should have slept; then I should have been at rest,

14 with kings and counselors of the earth
   who rebuilt ruins for themselves,

15 or with princes who had gold,
   who filled their houses with silver.

16 Or why was I not as a hidden untimely birth,
   as infants that never see the light?

17 There the wicked cease from troubling,
   and there the weary are at rest.

18 There the prisoners are at ease together;
   they hear not the voice of the taskmaster;

19 The small and the great are there,
   and the slave is free from his master."

(Revised Standard Version)

JOB 14.1–12

1 Man that is born of woman
   is of few days, and full of trouble.

2 He comes forth like a flower, and is cut down;
   he fleeth also as a shadow, and continueth not.

3 And dost thou open thy eyes upon such a one
   and bringest me into judgment with thee?

4 Who can bring a clean thing out of an unclean? Not one.

5 Seeing his days are determined,
   the number of his months are with thee.
   thou hast appointed his bounds that he cannot pass;

6 turn from him, that he may rest,
   till he shall accomplish, as a hireling, his day.

7 For there is hope of a tree,
    if it be cut down, that it will sprout again,
    and that the tender branch thereof will not cease.

8 Though the root thereof wax old in the earth,
    and the stock thereof die in the ground;

9 yet through the scent of water it will bud,
    and bring forth boughs like a plant.

10 But man dieth, and wasteth away;
    yea, man giveth up the ghost, and where is he?

11 As the waters fail from the sea,
    and the flood decayeth and drieth up;

12 so man lieth down, and riseth not;

(King James Version)

ECCLESIASTES

1.2–4. 2 Vanity of vanities, says the Preacher, vanity of vanities; all is vanity. 3 What does a man gain by all the toil at which he toils under the sun? 4 A generation comes, and a generation goes; but the earth remains for ever.

2.14–17. 14 The wise man has eyes in his head, but the fool walks in darkness; and yet I perceived that one fate comes to all of them. 15 Then I said to myself, "What befalls the fool will befall me also; why then have I been so very wise?" 16 And I said to myself that also is vanity. For of the wise man as of the fool there is no enduring remembrance, seeing that in the days to come all will have been long forgotten. How the wise man dies just like the fool! 17 So I hated life, because what is done under the sun was grievous to me; for all is vanity and a striving after wind.

3.18–22. 18 I said in my heart with regard to the sons of men that God is testing them to show them that they are but beasts. 19 For the fate of the sons of men and the fate of beasts is the same; as one dies, so dies the other. They all have the same breath, and man has no advantage over the beasts; for all is vanity. 20 All go to one place; all are from the dust, and all turn to dust again. 21 Who knows whether the spirit of man goes upward and the spirit of the beast goes down to the earth? 22 So I saw that there is nothing better than that a man should enjoy his work, for that is his lot; who can bring him to see what will be after him?

4.1–3. 1 Again I saw all the oppressions that are practiced under the sun. And behold the tears of the oppressed, and they had no one to comfort them! On the side of their oppressors there was power, and there was no one to comfort them. 2 And I thought the dead who are already dead more fortunate than the living who are still alive; 3 but better than both is he who has not yet been, and has not seen the evil deeds that are done under the sun.

9.2–6.2 One fate comes to all, to the righteous and the wicked, to the good and the evil, to the clean and the unclean, to him who sacrifices and him who does no sacrifice. As is the good man, so is the sinner; and he who swears is as he who shuns an oath. 3 This is an evil in all that is done under the sun, that one fate comes to all; also the hearts of men are full of evil, and madness is in their hearts while they live, and after that they go to the dead. 4 But he who is joined with all the living has hope, for a living dog is better than a dead lion. 5 For the living know that they will die, but the dead know nothing, and they have no more reward; but the memory of them is lost. 6 Their love and their hate and their envy have already perished, and they have no more for ever any share in all that is done under the sun.

9.9–10. 9 Enjoy life with the wife whom you love, all the days of your vain life, which he has given you under the sun, because that is your portion in life and in your toil at which you toil under the sun. 10 Whatever your hand finds to do, do it with your might; for there is no work or thought or knowledge or wisdom in Sheol, to which you are going.

11.7–8. 7 Light is sweet, and it is pleasant for the eyes to behold the sun. 8 For if a man lives many years, let him rejoice in them all; but let him remember that the days of darkness will be many. All that comes is vanity.

12.1–8. 1 Remember also your grave* in the days of your youth, before the evil days come, and the years draw nigh, when you will say, "I have no pleasure in them"; 2 before the suns and the light and the moon and the stars are darkened and the clouds return after the rain; 3 in the day when the keepers of the house tremble, and the strong men are bent, and the grinders cease because they are few, and those that look through the windows are dimmed, 4 and the doors on the street are shut; when the sound of the grinding is low, and one rises up at the

---

*Most translations read "Remember your Creator," but in Hebrew the words for "Creator" (*boreh*) and "grave" (bor) are practically identical, and the latter is more appropriate here.

voice of a bird, and all the daughters of song are brought low; 5 they are afraid also of what is high, and terrors are in the way; the almond tree blossoms, the grasshopper drags itself along and desire fails; because man goes to his eternal home, and the mourners go about the streets; 6 before the silver cord is snapped, or the golden bowl is broken, or the pitcher is broken at the fountain, or the wheel broken at the cistern, 7 and the dust returns to the dust as it was, and the spirit returns to God who gave it. 8 Vanity of vanities, says the Preacher, all is vanity.

HOMER
(EIGHTH CENTURY B.C.E.)

Homer, the first and greatest poet of classical antiquity, is also one of its greatest mortalists. The death that awaits all his characters, from tragic heroes like Hector to drunken losers like Elpenor, is eternal, even though they do not, strictly speaking, undergo annihilation. As we see in Book XI of the *Odyssey* the dead have lead a pallid, shadowy existence, like moths in an attic, i.e., with no life of their own, merely as the object, at best, of the memory of the living. The gods in both the *Iliad* and the *Odyssey* have it easy, banqueting on Mount Olympus, fêted and sacrificed to by humans, who live and die by the gods' caprice and the random strokes of fate. In our first scene, on the battlefield before Troy the Trojan Glaucus meets Diomedes, who asks about his lineage; the second scene describes the death of Zeus's son Sarpedon; and the third dramatizes the encounter between Achilles and Priam at the end of the *Iliad*. In the final excerpt Odysseus encounters the wraith of his mother Antikleia in Hades.

A word about Alexander Pope's translation: though strikingly rhetorical, artificial, and sometimes marred by operatic hyperbole, it is no doubt the grandest English version of Homer and a brilliant attempt to convey the range of emotions suggested by the elusive term "heroic." The much humbler prose version of the passage from the *Odyssey* by the Victorian satirist and polymath, Samuel Butler (who incidentally maintained that the *Odyssey* was written by a woman) manages to convey the quiet eloquence and understated pathos of Homer that Pope often had to sacrifice.

GLAUCUS ("THE CHIEF") AND DIOMEDES ("TYDEUS' SON")

What, or from whence I am, or who my Sire,
(Reply'd the Chief) can Tydeus' Son enquire?
Like Leaves on Trees the Race of Man is found,
Now green in Youth, now with'ring on the Ground,
Another Race the following Spring supplies,
They fall successive, and successive rise;

So generations in their Course decay,
So flourish these, when those are past away.

VI.169–176

THE DEATH OF SARPEDON

When now Sarpedon his brave Friends beheld
Grov'ling in Dust, and gasping on the Field,
With this Reproach his flying Host he warms,
Oh Stain to Honour! Oh Disgrace to Arms!
Forsake, inglorious this contended Plain;
This Hand, unaided, shall the War sustain:
The task be mine this Hero's strength to try,
Who mows whole Troops, and makes an Army fly.
    He spake; and speaking, leaps from off the Car;   520
Patroclus lights, and sternly waits the War.

* * *

As when two Vultures on the Mountains's Height
Stoop with re-sounding Pinions to the Fight;
They cuff, they tear, they raise a screaming Cry;
The Desert echoes, and the Rocks reply:
The Warriors thus oppos'd in Arms, engage
With equal Clamours, and with equal Rage.
    Jove view'd the Combate, whose Event foreseen,
He thus bespoke his Sister and his Queen.
The Hour draws on, the Destinies ordain,   530
My godlike Son shall press the Phrygian Plain:
Already on the Verge of Death he stands,
His life is ow'd to fierce Patroclus' Hands.
What Passions in a parent's Breast debate!
Say, shall I snatch him from impending Fate,
And send him safe to Lycia, distant far
From all the Dangers and the Toils of War;
Or to his Doom my bravest Offspring yield,
And fatten, with celestial Blood, the Field?
    Then thus the Goddess with the radiant Eyes: 540
What Words are these, O Sov'reign of the Skies?
Short is the Date prescrib'd to mortal Man;

Shall Jove, for one, extend the narrow Span,
Whose Bounds were fix'd before his Race began?
How many Sons of Gods, foredoom'd to Death,
Before proud Ilion, must resign their Breath!
Were thine exempt, Debate would rise above,
And murm'ring Pow'rs condemn their partial Jove,
Give the bold Chief a glorious Fate in fight;
And when th'ascending Soul has wing'd her flight,   550
Let Sleep and Death convey, by thy Command,
The breathless Body to his native Land.
His Friends and People, to his future Praise,
A marble Tomb and Pyramid shall raise,
And lasting Honours to his Ashes give;
His Fame ('tis all the Dead can have) shall live.
    She said; the Cloud-compeller overcome,
Assents to Fate, and ratifies the Doom.
Then touch'd with Grief, the weeping Heav'ns distill'd
A Show'r of Blood o'er all the fatal Field.   560
The God, his Eyes averting from the Plain,
Laments his Son, predestin'd to be slain,
Far from the Lycian Shores, his happy native Reign.
Now met in Arms, the Combatants appear,
Each heav'd the Shield, and pois'd the lifted Spear:
From strong Patroclus' Hand the Javelin fled,
And pass'd the Groin of valiant Thrasymed.
The Nerves unbrac'd no more his Bulk sustain,
He falls, and falling bites the Plain.
Two sounding Darts the Lycian Leader threw;
The first aloof with erring Fury flew,
The next transpierc'd Achilles mortal Steed,
The gen'rous Pedasus, of Theban Breed;
Fix'd in the Shoulders Joint, he reel'd around;
Rowl'd in the bloody dust, and paw'd the slip'ry Ground.

* * *

The tow'ring Chiefs to fiercer Fight advance
And first Sarpedon whirl'd his weighty Lance,
Which o'er the Warrior's Shoulder took its Course
And spent in empty Air its dying Force,
Not so Patroclus' never erring Dart;
Aim'd at his Breast, it pierc'd the mortal Part

Where the strong Fibres bind the solid Heart.   590
Then, as the Mountain Oak, or Poplar tall
Or Pine (fit Mast for some great Admiral)
Nods to the Axe, till with a groaning Sound
It sinks, and spreads its Honours on the Ground;
Thus fell the King; and laid on Earth supine,
Before his Chariot stretch'd his Form divine:
He gasp'd the Dust distain'd with streaming Gore,
And pale in Death, lay groaning on the Shore.
So lies a Bull beneath the Lion's Paws,   600
While the grim Savage grinds with foamy Jaws
The trembling Limbs, and sucks the smoaking Blood;
Deep groans and hollow roars, rebellow thro' the Wood,
      Then to the Leader of the Lycian Band
The dying Chief address'd his last Command.
Glaucus, be bold; thy Task be first to dare
The glorious Dangers of destructive War,
To lead my Troops, to combate at their Head,
Incite the Living, and supply the Dead.
Tell 'em, I charg'd them with my latest Breath
Not unaveng'd to bear Sarpedon's death.   610
What Grief, what Shame must Glaucus undergo,
If these spoil'd Arms adorn a Grecian Foe?
Then as a Friend, and as a Warrior, fight;
Defend my Corpse, and conquer in my Right;
That taught by great Examples, all may try
Like thee to vanquish, or like me to die.
      He ceas'd; the Fates suppress'd his lab'ring Breath,
And his Eyes darken'd with the Shades of Death
Th' insulting Victor with Disdain bestrode
The prostrate Prince, and on his Bosom trod;   620
Then drew the Weapon from his panting Heart,
The reeking Fibres clinging to the Dart;
From the wide Wound gush'd out a Stream of Blood,
And the Soul issu'd in the purple Flood.

* * *

      Now great Sarpedon, on the sandy Shore,
His heavn'ly Form defac'd with Dust and Gore,
And stuck with Darts by warring Heroes shed;
Lies undistinguish'd from the vulgar dead.

His long disputed Corpse the Chiefs inclose,
On ev'ry side the busy Combate grows;
Thick, as beneath some Shepherd's thatch'd Abode,
The Pails high-foaming with a milky Flood,   780
The buzzing Flies, a persevering Train,
Incessant swarm, and chas'd, return again.
    Jove view'd the Combate with a stern Survey,
And Eyes that flash'd intolerable Day;
Fix'd on the Field, his Breast debates
The Vengeance due, and meditates the Fates;
Whether to urge their prompt Effect, and call
The Force of Hector to Patroclus' Fall,
This Instant see his short-liv'd trophies won,
And stretch him breathless on his slaughter'd Son;   790
Or yet, with many a Soul's untimely flight,
Augment the Fame and Horror of the Fight?
To crown Achilles; valiant Friend with Praise
At length he dooms; and that his last of Days
Shall set in Glory, bids him drive the Foe;
Nor unattended, see the Shades below.
Then Hector's Mind he fills with dire Dismay;
He mounts his Car, and calls his Hosts away;
Sunk with Troy's heavy Fates, he sees decline
The Scales of Jove, and pants with Awe divine.   800

* * *

    Then thus to Phoebus, in the Realms above,
Spoke from his Throne the Cloud-compelling Jove.   810
Descend, my Phoebus! On the Phrygian Plain,
And from the Fight convey Sarpedon slain;
Then bathe his Body in the crystal Flood,
With Dust dishonour'd, and deform'd with Blood:
O'er all his Limbs Ambrosial Odours shed,
And with celestial Robes adorn the Dead.
Those Rites discharg'd, his sacred Copse bequeath
To the soft Arms of silent Sleep and Death;
They to his Friends the mournful Charge shall bear,
His Friends a Tomb and Pyramid shall rear;   820
What Honours Mortals after Death receive,
Those unavailing Honours we may give!
Apollo bows, and from Mount Ida's Height,

Swift to the Field precipitates his Flight;
Thence from the War the breathless Hero bore,
Veil'd in a Cloud, to silver Simois' Shore:
There bath'd his honourable Wounds, and drest
His manly Members in th'immortal Vest;
And with Perfumes of sweet Ambrosial Dews,
Restores his Freshness, and his Form renews.   830
Then Sleep and Death, two Twins of winged Race,
Of matchless Swiftness, but of silent Pace,
Receiv'd Sarpedon, at the God's Command,
And in a Moment reach'd the Lycian Land;
The Corpse amidst his weeping Friends they laid,
Where Endless Honours wait the sacred Shade.

ACHILLES AND PRIAM

Each look'd on other, none the Silence broke,
Till thus at last the Kingly Suppliant spoke.
Ah think, thou favour'd of the Pow'rs Divine!
Think of thy Father's Age, and pity mine!
In me, that Father's rev'rend Image trace,   600
Those silver Hairs, that venerable Face;
His trembling Limbs, his helpless Person, see!
In all my Equal, but in Misery!
Yet now perhaps, some Turn of Human Fate
Expells him helpless from his peaceful State;
Think from some pow'rful Foe thou see'st him fly,
And beg Protection with a feeble Cry,
Yet still one Comfort in his Soul may rise;
He hears his Son still lives to glad his Eyes;
And hearing still may hope a better Day   610
May send him thee to chase that Foe away.
No Comfort to my Griefs, no Hopes remain,
The best, the bravest of my Sons are slain!
Still One was left, their Loss to recompense;
His Father's Hope, his Country's last Defence.
Him too thy Rage has slain! Beneath thy Steel   620
Unhappy in his Country's Cause he fell!
   Think of thy Father, and this face behold!
See him in me, as helpless and as old!
Tho' not so wretched: There he yields to me,

The First of Men in sov'reign Misery.
Thus forc'd to kneel, thus grov'ling to embrace
The Scourge and Ruin of my Realm and Race;
Suppliant my Childrens Murd'rer to implore,
And kiss those Hands yet reeking with their Gore!

* * *

Satiate at length with unavailing Woes,
From the high Throne divine Achilles rose;
The rev'rend Monarch by the Hand he rais'd;
On his white Beard and Form majestick gaz'd,   650
Not unrelenting: Then serene began
With Words to sooth the miserable Man,
        Alas! What Weight of Anguish hast thou known?
Unhappy Prince! Thus guardless and alone
To pass thro' Foes, and thus undaunted face
The Man whose Fury has destroy'd thy Race?
Heav'n sure has arm'd thee with a Heart of Steel,
A Strength proportion'd to the Woes you feel.
Rise then: Let Reason mitigate our Care:
To mourn, avails not: Man is born to bear.   660
Such is, alas! The Gods severe decree;
They, only they are blest, and only free.
Two Urns by Jove's high Throne have ever stood,
The Source of Evil one, and one of Good;
From thence the Cup of mortal Man he fills,
Blessings to these, to those distributes Ills;
To most, he mingles both: The Wretch decreed
To taste the bad, unmix'd, is curst indeed;
Pursu'd by Wrongs, by meager Famine driv'n,
He wanders, Outcast both of Earth and Heav'n.   670
The Happiest taste not Happiness sincere,
But find the cordial Draught is dash'd with Care.
Who more than Peleus shone in Wealth and Pow'r?
What Stars concurring blest his natal Hour?
A Realm, a Goddess, to his Wishes giv'n,
Grac'd by the Gods with all the Gifts of Heav'n!
One Evil yet o'ertakes his latest Day,
No Race succeeding to imperial Sway:
One only Son! And he (alas!) ordain'd
To fall untimely in a foreign Land!   680

See him, in Troy, the pious Care decline
Of his weak Age, to live the Cause of thine!
    Thou too, Old Man, hast happier Days beheld;
In Riches once, in Children once excell'd;
Extended Phrygia own'd thy ample Reign,
And all fair Lesbos' blissful Seats contain,
And all wide Hellespont's unmeasur'd Main.
    But since the God has pleas'd to turn,
And fill thy Measure from his bitter Urn,
What sees the Sun, but hapless Heroes Falls?   690
War, and the Blood of Men, surround thy Walls!
What must be, must be. Bear thy Lot, nor shed
These unavailing Sorrows o'er the Dead;
Thou can'st not call him from the Stygian Shore,
But thou alas! May'st live to suffer more.

                    (trans. Alexander Pope [1715–1720])

ODYSSEUS MEETS HIS MOTHER ANTIKLEIA IN HADES

On this the ghost of Tiresias went back to the house of Hades, for his prophesy-
ings had now been spoken, but I sat still where I was until my mother came up
and tasted the blood. Then she knew me at once and spoke fondly to me, saying,
"My son, how did you come down to this abode of darkness while you are still
alive? It is a hard thing for the living to see these places, for between us and them
there are great and terrible waters, and there is Oceanus, which no man can cross
on foot, but he must have a good ship to take him. Are you all this time trying to
find your way home from Troy, and have you never got back to Ithaca nor seen
your wife in your own house?"

    "Mother," said I, "I was forced to come here to consult the ghost of the
Theban prophet Tiresias. I have never yet been near the Achaean land nor set foot
on my native country, and I have had nothing but one long series of misfortunes
from the very first day that I set out for Ilium, the land of noble steeds, to fight
the Trojans. But tell me, and tell me true, in what way did you die? Did you have
a long illness, or did heaven vouchsafe you a gentle easy passage to eternity? Tell
me also about my father, and the son whom I left behind me. Is my property still
in their hands, or has some one else got hold of it, who thinks that I shall not
return to claim it? Tell me again what my wife intends doing, and in what mind
she is; does she live with my son and guard my estate securely, or has she made
the best match she could and married again?"

    My mother answered, "Your wife still remains in your house, but she is in
great distress of mind and spends her whole time in tears both night and day. No

one as yet has got possession of your fine property, and Telemachus still holds your lands undisturbed. He has to entertain largely, as of course he must, considering his position as a magistrate, and how every one invites him; your father remains at his old place in the country and never comes near the town. He has no comfortable bed nor bedding; in the winter he sleeps on the floor in front of the fire with the men and goes about all in rags, but in summer, when the warm weather comes on again, he lies out in the vineyard on a bed of vine leaves thrown any how upon the ground. He grieves continually about your never having come home, and suffers more and more as he grows older. As for my own end it was in this wise: heaven did not take me swiftly and painlessly in my own house, nor was I attacked by any illness such as those that generally wear people out and kill them, but my longing to know what you were doing, and the force of my affection for you—this it was that was the death of me."

Then I tried to find some way of embracing my poor mother's ghost. Thrice I sprang towards her and tried to clasp her in my arms, but each time she flitted from my embrace as it were a dream or phantom, and being touched to the quick, I said to her, "Mother, why do you not stay still when I would embrace you? If we could throw our arms around one another we might find comfort in the sharing of our sorrows even in the house of Hades; does Proserpine want to lay a still further load of grief upon me by mocking me with a phantom only?"

"My son," she answered, "most ill-fated of mankind, it is not Proserpine that is beguiling you, but all people are like this when they are dead. The sinews no longer hold the flesh and bones together; these perish in the fierceness of consuming fire as soon as life has left the body, and the soul flits away as though it was a dream. Now, however, go back to the light of day as you can, and note all these things that may tell them to your wife hereafter."

(trans. Samuel Butler [1900])

SOPHOCLES (496–406 B.C.E.)

Perhaps the lowest note in the gamut of mortalism is the notion that not only do we die forever, but that, all things considered, it would have been better for us never to have been born: an impossible and useless sentiment, of course, since anyone voicing it or hearing it is already trapped. The idea receives its most famous expression in the following lines, where the Chorus (itself made up of old men) in *Oedipus at Colonus*, shaken by its encounter with the blinded, exiled, miserable Oedipus, reflects that the game just wasn't worth the candle. Since *Oedipus at Colonus* was written at the end of Sophocles' very long life, this ode inevitably sounds like a personal confession.

CHORUS FROM *OEDIPUS AT COLONUS*

What man is he that yearneth
For length unmeasured of days?
Folly mine eye discerneth
    Encompassing all his ways,
For years over-running the measure
    Shall change thee in evil wise:
Grief draweth nigh thee; and pleasure,
    Behold, it is hid from thine eyes.
    This is their wage have they
    Which overlive their day.

And He that looseth from labour
    Doth one with other befriend,
    Whom bride nor bridesmen attend,
Song, nor sound of the tabor,
    Death that maketh an end.

Thy portion esteem I highest,
    Who wast not ever begot;

Thine next, being born who diest
   And straightway again thou art not.
With follies light as the feather
   Doth Youth to man befall;
Then evils gather together,
     There wants not one of them all—
   Wrath, envy, discord, strife,
   The sword that seeketh life.
And sealing the sum of trouble
   Doth suffering Age draw nigh,
   Whom friends and kinsfolk fly,
Age, upon whom redouble
   All sorrows under the sky.
This man, as me, even so,
Have the evil days overtaken;
And like as a cape sea-shaken
With tempest at earth's last verges

And shock of all winds that blow,
His head the seas of woe,
The thunders of awful surges
Ruining overflow;
Blown from the fall of even,
   Blown from the dayspring forth,
Blown from the noon in heaven,
   Blown from night and the North.

                   (trans. A. E. Housman)

OTHER GREEK POETS

The theme of mortalism in ancient Greek poetry is so strong that this section could be extended ad infinitum. Here are a few brief examples. Note that shorter poems in the classical age were not given titles.

ANACREON (CA. 570–500 B.C.E.)

I have gone gray at the temples,
yes, my head is white, there's nothing
of the grace of youth that's left me,
and my teeth are like an old man's.
Life is lovely. But the lifetime
that remains for me is little.
For this cause I mourn. The terrors
of the Dark Pit never leave me.
For the house of Death is deep down
underneath, the downward journey
to be feared, for once I go there
I know well there's no returning.

(trans. Richmond Lattimore)

THEOGNIS (SIXTH CENTURY B.C.E.)

Best of all things—is never to be born,
never to know the light of sharp sun.
But being born, then best
to pass quickly as one can through the gates of Hell,
and there lie under the massive shield of earth.

(trans. Willis Barnstone)

ANYTE (FOURTH CENTURY B.C.E.)

When this man, Manes, lived, he was a slave,
Dead he is worth as much as Darius the Great.

(trans. Sally Purcell)

CALLIMACHUS (310–240 B.C.E.)

"Is Kháridas beneath this stone?"
"Yes, if you mean Arrímas's son
from Kyréne, I'm his tomb."

"Kháridas, what's it like below?"
"Dark." "Are there exits?" "None."
"And Pluto?" "He's a myth." "Oh, no!"

"All that I'm telling you is true,
But if you want the bright side too,
The cost of living here is low."

(trans. Stanley Lombardo and Diane Rayor)

They told me, Heraclitus, they told me you were dead,
They brought me bitter news to hear and bitter tears to shed.
I wept as I remember'd how often you and I
Had tired the sun with talking and sent him down the sky.

And now that thou art lying, my dear old Carian guest,
A handful of grey ashes, long, long ago at rest,
Still are thy pleasant voices, thy nightingales awake;
For Death, he taketh all away, but them he cannot take.

(trans. Henry Cory [1858])

DIOTIMUS (THIRD CENTURY B.C.E.)

Homeward at evening through the drifted snow
The cows plod back to shelter from the hill
But ah, the long strange sleep

Of the cow-herd Therimachos lying beneath the oak,
Struck still, still, by the fire that falls from heaven.

(trans. Dudley Fitts)

MOSCHUS (FL. CA. 150 B.C.E.)

Ah! When the mallow in the croft dies down,
Or the pale parsley or the crisped anise,
Again they grow, another year they flourish;
But we, the great, the valiant, and the wise,
Once covered over in the hollow earth,
Sleep a long, dreamless, unawakening sleep.

(trans. Walter Savage Landor [1842])

PAULUS SILENTIARIUS (SIXTH CENTURY C.E.)

My name was—(Well—what signifies?)—my nation—
(Well, what of that?)—my birth and education—
(Were good or bad; of course—no matter which)
My life—(Well, sink all that—was poor or rich)—
Who cares?)—I died, aged—(Oh, drop that stuff)
And here I lie—(Ay, ay—that's sure enough.)

(trans. Leigh Hunt [1837])

PLATO (428–348 B.C.E.)

Sometimes the strongest arguments against an idea come from its supporters. Plato, who must be rated one of supreme *im*mortalists, nevertheless has his hero and mouthpiece Socrates admit in the *Apology*:

> One of two things: either death is a state of nothingness and utter unconscious-ness or, *as men say* [my emphasis], there is a change and migration of the soul from this world to another. Now if you suppose that there is no consciousness, but a sleep like the sleep of him who is undisturbed even by the sight of dreams, death will be an unspeakable gain. For if a person were to select the night in which his sleep was undisturbed even by dreams, and were to compare with this the other days and nights of his life, and then were to tell us how many days and nights he had passed in the course of his life better and more pleasantly than this one, I think that any man, I will not say a private man, but even the great king [of Persia], would not find many such days or nights, when compared with the others. Now if death is like this, I say that to die is gain; for eternity is then only a single night.
>
> (40D–E; trans. Benjamin Jowett)

Then in the *Phaedo*, the great Platonic dialogue on the immortality of the soul, Socrates discusses the afterlife with his friends on the very day when he himself is about to be executed. So confident is Plato of his case that he has two of those friends raise devastating objections: Simmias presents the Pythagorean notion that the soul is an epiphenomenon of the body, like the tuning of a musical instrument, which cannot survive the destruction of that instrument. Cebes concedes that the soul may have preexisted the body and may survive one or more reincarnations, but he argues that, like a human being who wears out many garments before dying himself, the soul might well perish in the end. Socrates' responses, not given here, do not seriously dent these objections.

[Simmias]: When I consider the matter either alone or with Cebes, the argument does certainly appear to me, Socrates, to be not sufficient.

Socrates answered: I dare say, my friend, that you may be right, but I should like to know in what respect the argument is not sufficient.

In this respect, replied Simmias: Might not a person use the same argument about harmony and the lyre—might he not say that harmony is a thing invisible, incorporeal, fair, divine, abiding in the lyre which is harmonized, but that the lyre and the strings are matter and material, composite, earthy, and akin to mortality? And when someone breaks the lyre, or cuts and rends the strings, then he who takes this view would argue as you do, and on the same analogy, that the harmony survives and has not perished; for you cannot imagine, as we would say, that the lyre without the strings, and the broken strings themselves, remain, and yet that the harmony, which is of heavenly and immortal nature and kindred, has perished—and perished too before the mortal. The harmony, he would say, certainly exists somewhere, and the wood and strings will decay before that decays. For I suspect, Socrates, that the notion of the soul which we are all of us inclined to entertain, would also be yours, and that you too would conceive the body to be strung up, and held together, by the elements of hot and cold, wet and dry, and the like, and that the soul is the harmony or due proportionate admixture of them. And if this is true, the inference clearly is that when the strings of the body are unduly loosened or overstrained through disorder or other injury, then the soul, though most divine, like other harmonies of music or of the works of art, of course perishes at once, although the material remains of the body may last for a considerable time, until they are either decayed or burnt. Now if anyone maintained that the soul, being the harmony of the elements of the body, first perishes in that which is called death, how shall we answer him?

Socrates looked around at us as his manner was, and said, with a smile: Simmias has reason on his side; and why does not some one of you who is abler than myself answer him? For there is force in his attack on me. But perhaps, before we answer him, we had best also hear what Cebes has to say against the argument—this will give us time for reflection, and when both of them have spoken, we may either assent to them if their words appear to be in consonance with the truth, or if not, we may take up the other side and argue with them. Please to tell me, then, Cebes, he said, what was the difficulty which troubled you?

Cebes said: I will tell you . . . I am ready to admit that the existence of the soul before entering into the body form has been very ingeniously, and, as I may be allowed to say, quite sufficiently proven; but the existence of the soul after death is still, in my judgment, unproven. Now my objection is not the same as that of Simmias; for I am not disposed to deny that the soul is stronger and more lasting than the body, being of the opinion that in all such respects the soul very far excels the body. Well, then, says the argument to me, why do you remain unconvinced? When you see that the weaker is still in existence after the man is dead, will you not admit that the more lasting must also survive during the same period of time? Now I, like Simmias, must employ a figure; and I shall ask you to consider whether the figure is to the point. The parallel which I will suppose is that of an old weaver, who dies, and after his death somebody says: he is not dead, he must be alive; and he appeals to the coat which he himself wove and wore, and which is still whole and undecayed. And then he proceeds to ask of someone who is incredulous, whether a man lasts longer, or the coat which is in use and wear; and when he is answered that a man lasts far longer, thinks that he has certainly demonstrated the survival of the man, who is the more lasting, because the less lasting remains. But that, Simmias, as I would beg you to observe, is not the truth; everyone sees that he who talks thus is talking nonsense. For the truth is that this weaver, having worn and woven many such coats, though he outlived several of them, was himself outlived by the last; but this is surely very far from proving that a man is slighter and weaker than a coat. Now the relation of the body to the soul may be expressed in a similar figure; for you may say with reason that the soul is lasting, and the body weak and short-lived in comparison. And every soul may be said to wear out many bodies, especially in the course of a long life. For if while the man is alive the body deliquesces and decays, and yet the soul always weaves her garment anew and repairs the waste, then, of course, when the soul perishes, she must have on her last garment, and this only will survive her; but then again when the soul is dead the body will at last show its native weakness, and soon pass into decay. And therefore this is an argument on which I would rather not rely as proving that the soul exists after death. For suppose that we grant even more than you affirm as within the range of possibility, and besides acknowledging that the soul existed before birth admit also that after death the souls of some are existing still, and will exist, and will be born and die again and again, and that there is a natural strength in the soul which will hold out and be born many times—for all this, we may be still inclined to think that she will weary in the labors of successive births, and may at last succumb in one of her deaths and utterly perish; and this death and dissolution of the body which brings destruction to the soul may be unknown to any of us, for no one of us can have had any experience of it; and if this is true, then I say that he who is confident in death has but a foolish confidence, unless he is able to prove that the soul is altogether immortal and imperishable. But if he is not able to do this, he who is about to die will always have reason to fear that when the body is disunited, the soul also may utterly perish.

All of us, as we afterwards remarked to one another, had an unpleasant feeling at hearing them say this. When we had been so firmly convinced before, now to have our faith shaken seemed to introduce a confusion and uncertainty, not only into the previous argument but into any future one; either we were not good judges, or there were no real grounds of belief.

(85D–88C; trans. Benjamin Jowett [1871])

EPICURUS (341–270 B.C.E.)

Epicurus is the most important figure in the history of mortalism, but not because he left any philosophical masterpieces behind. As David John Furley says, "Apart from the letter to Menoeceus [part of which is given below], and a few of the maxims, Epicurus' surviving writings are needlessly difficult, clumsy, ambiguous, badly organized, and full of jargon. Present-day knowledge and appreciation of Epicurus' system depends very largely on the poem of Lucretius, *De rerum natura*" (*Oxford Classical Dictionary*, 2d ed., p. 391). We will be getting to Lucretius shortly, but in the meantime a letter from his master is included here:

LETTER TO MENOECEUS

Get used to the idea that death means nothing to us, since everything good and evil consists in perception, but death removes all perception. And so a correct understanding that death is nothing to us makes the fact that life ends in death enjoyable, not because it adds on an infinite period of time, but because it takes away the yearning for immortality. For there is nothing terrible in life for the man who has truly understood that there is nothing terrible in not being alive. A man is a fool, then, if he says that he fears death not because it will be painful when it arrives, but because it will be painful in the process of coming. Because anything that causes no trouble when it's present is just an empty source of pain when merely anticipated. Thus death, which is the most frightening of evils, is nothing to us, insofar as when we exist, there is no death; but when death is present, *we* don't exist. It is of no concern, then, to either the living or the dead, since for the first it doesn't exist, and for the second, they no longer exist. Yet the majority sometimes flee death as the greatest of evils, and sometimes long for it as relief from the evils of life. But the wise man neither begs off from life nor does he fear the loss of it. For life does not offend him, nor does not being alive seem an evil to him. And just as he doesn't automatically choose the largest amount of food, but the tastiest dish, he doesn't grasp for the longest span of time but the most pleasant one.

Meanwhile, a person who advises the young to live well and the old to end well is a simpleton, not just because life is welcome, but because the same practice teaches us both how to live well and how to die well. Much worse is the person who claims it is good never to have been born and, once born, to pass through the gates of Hades as quickly as possible. For if he really believes what he says, why doesn't he just take his leave of life? After all, this option is ready to hand if he has firmly decided to take it.

(trans. Peter Heinegg)

TITUS LUCRETIUS CARUS
(92?–55 B.C.E.)

L ucretius is the king of mortalists. A disciple of Epicurus, whom he adulated, he presents a grand exposition of his master's teachings in *De rerum natura* (On the Nature of Things), quite possibly the greatest philosophical poem ever written. In it Lucretius defends a thorough-going materialism, including the materiality of the soul, which is born, evolves, and dies with the body. He cites the instances of drunkenness and epilepsy to show how the mind is affected by our physical condition, and continues his onslaught against the notion of a disembodied spirit existing either before or after the life of the body. Lucretius aims at uprooting the superstitious terrors of Hades and the world beyond death, while urging humans to concentrate on the rational purpose of life: pleasure (in moderation). Over two millenia after they were written, his lines still astonish us with their clarity, calm logic, and authority.

If there is a problem with this magisterial figure, it may well be his lack of sympathy for the poor, confused mortals whom he's trying to help: like Epicurus before him and Marcus Aurelius after him, he doesn't seem to appreciate the fact that in some cases death can be a shattering agony, both for the victim and the survivors. Lucretius' propagandistic aim succeeds so splendidly that other features of death become obscured. John Dryden's translation (1685) of part of Book III of *De rerum natura* (into the inevitable heroic couplet) is hasty but vigorous, sprawling but hearty, sloppy but supremely alive.

FROM BOOK III OF *DE RERUM NATURA*

What has this bugbear, death, to frighten man,
If souls can die, as well as bodies can?
For, as before our birth we felt no pain,
When Punic arms* infested land and main,
When heaven and earth were in confusion hurled,   5

---

*Wars with Carthage from 264–241, 218–201, and 149–146 B.C.E.

41

For the debated empire of the world,
Which awed with dreadful expectation lay,
Sure to be slaves, uncertain who should sway:
So, when our mortal flame shall be disjoined,
The lifeless lump uncoupled from the mind,   10
From sense of grief and pain we shall be free;
We shall not feel, because we shall not be.
Though earth in seas, and seas in heav'n were lost,
We should not move, we only should be tossed.
Nay, ev'n suppose, when we have suffered fate,   15
The soul could feel in her divided state,
What's that to us? For we are only we,
While souls and bodies in one frame agree.
Nay, though our atoms should revolve by chance,
And matter leap into the former dance;   20
Though time our life and motion could restore,
And make our bodies what they were before;

What gain to us would all this bustle bring?
The new-made man would be another thing.
When once an interrupting pause is made,   25
That individual being is decayed.
We, who are dead and gone, shall bear no part
In all the pleasures, nor shall feel the smart,
Which to that other mortal shall accrue,
Whom of our matter time shall mould anew.   30
For backward if you look on that long space
Of ages past, and view the changing face
Of matter, tossed and variously combined
In sundry shapes, 'tis easy for the mind
From thence t' infer, that seeds of things have been   35
In the same order as they now are seen;
Which yet our dark remembrance cannot trace,
Because a pause of life, a gaping space,
Has come betwixt, where memory lies dead,
And all the wandering motions from the sense are fed.   40
For whosoe'er shall in misfortunes live,
Must *be*, when those misfortunes shall arrive;
And since the man who *is* not, feels not woe,
(For death exempts him, and wards off the blow,
Which we, the living, only feel and bear,)   45
What is there for us in death to fear?

When once that pause of life has come between,
'Tis just the same as we had never been.

And, therefore, if a man bemoan his lot,
That after death his moldering limbs shall rot,   50
Or flames or jaws of beasts devour his mass,
Know, he's an insincere, unthinking ass,
A secret sting remains within his mind;
The fool is to his own cast offals kind.
He boasts no sense can after death remain;   55
Yet makes himself a part of life again,
As if some other *he* could feel the pain,
If, while we live, this thought molest his head,
"What wolf or vulture shall devour me dead?"
He wastes his days in idle grief, nor can   60
Distinguish 'twixt the body and the man;
But thinks himself can still himself survive,
And, what when dead he feels not, feels alive.
Then he repines that he was born to die,
Nor knows in death there is no other He,   65
No living He remains his grief to vent,
And o'er his senseless carcass to lament.
If, after death, 'tis painful to be torn
By birds and beasts, then why not so to burn,
Or drenched in floods of honey to be soaked,   70
Imbalm'd to be at once preserved and choked;
Or on an airy mountain's top to lie,
Exposed to cold and heav'n's inclemency;
Or crowded in a tomb, to be oppressed
With monumental marble on thy breast?   75
But to be snatched from all the household joys,
From thy chaste wife, and thy dear prattling boys,
Whose little arms about thy legs are cast,
And climbing for a kiss prevent their mother's haste,
Inspiring secret pleasure through thy breast;   80
Ah! These shall be no more; thy friends oppressed
Thy care and courage now no more shall free;
"Ah! Wretch!," thou criest, "ah! Miserable me!
One woeful day sweeps children, friends and wife,
And all the brittle blessings of my life!"   85
Add one thing more, and all thou say'st is true;
Thy want and wish of them is vanished too;

Which, well considered, were a quick relief
To all thy vain imaginary grief:
For thou shalt sleep, and never wake again,   90
And, quitting life, shall quit thy living pain.
But we, thy friends, shall all those sorrows find,
Which in forgetful death thou leav'st behind;
No time shall dry our tears, nor drive thee from our mind.
The worst that can befall thee, measured right,   95
Is a sound slumber, and a long good-night,
Yet thus the fools, that would be thought the wits,
Disturb their mirth with melancholy fits;
When healths go round, and kindly brimmers flow,
Till the fresh garlands on their foreheads glow,   100
They whine, and cry, "Let us make haste to live,
Short are the joys that human life can give,"
Eternal preachers, that corrupt the draught,
And pall the god, that never thinks, with thought;
Idiots, with all that thought, to whom the worst   105
Of death, is want of drink and endless thirst,
Or any fond desire as vain as these.
For, even in sleep, the body, wrapped in ease,
Supinely lies, as in the peaceful grave;
And, wanting nothing, nothing can it crave.   110
Were that sound sleep eternal, it were death;
Yet the first atoms then, the seeds of breath,
Are moving near to sense; we do but shake
And rouse that sense, and straight we are awake,
Then death to us, and death's anxiety,   115
Is less than nothing, if a less could be;
For then our atoms, which in order lay,
Are scattered from their heap, and puffed away,
And never can return into their place,
When once the pause of life has left an empty space,   120
And, last, suppose great nature's voice should call
To thee, or me, or any of us all,—
"What dost thou mean, ungrateful wretch, thou vain,
Thou mortal thing, thus idly to complain,
And sigh, and sob, that thou shalt be no more?   125
For, if thy life were pleasant heretofore,
If all the bounteous blessings I could give,
Thou hast enjoyed, if thou hast known to live,
And pleasure not leaked through thee like a sieve;

Why dost thou not give thanks as at a plenteous feast,   130
Crammed to the throat with life, and rise and take thy rest?
But, if my blessings thou has thrown away,
If undigested joys passed through, and would not stay,
Why dost thou wish for more to squander still?
If life be grown a load, a real ill,   135
And I would all thy cares and labours end,
Lay down thy burden, fool, and know thy friend.
To please thee, I have emptied all my store;
I can invent, and can supply no more,
But run the round again, the round I ran before.   140
Suppose thou art not broken yet with years,
Yet still the self-same scene of things appears,
And would be ever, couldst thou ever live;
For life is still but life, there's nothing new to give."
What can we plead against so just a bill?   145
We stand convicted, and our cause goes ill,
But if a wretch, a man oppressed by fate,
Should beg of nature to prolong his date,
She speaks aloud to him with more disdain.—
"Be still, thou martyr fool, thou covetous of pain,"   150
But if an old decrepit sot lament,—
"What, thou!" she cries, "who hast outlived content!
Dost thou complain, who has enjoyed my store?
But this is still the effect of wishing more.
Unsatisfied with all that nature brings;   155
Loathing the present, liking absent things;
From hence it comes, thy vain desires, at strife
Within themselves, have tantalised thy life,
And ghastly death appeared before thy sight,
Ere thou hast gorged thy soul and sense with delight.   160
Now leave these joys unsuiting to thy age,
To a fresh comer and resign the stage."
Is Nature to be blamed if thus she chide?
No, sure; for 'tis her business to provide
Against this ever-changing frame's decay,   165
New things to come, and old to pass away.
One being, worn, another being makes;
Changed, but not lost; for nature gives and takes:
New matter must be found for things to come,
And these must waste like those, and follow Nature's doom.   170
All things, like thee, have time to rise and rot,

And from each other's ruin are begot;
For life is not confined to him or thee;
'Tis given to all for use, to none for property.
Consider former ages past and gone,   175
Whose circles ended long ere thine begun,
Then tell me, fool, what part in them thou hast?
Thus may'st thou judge the future by the past.
What horror sees thou in that quiet state,
What bugbear dreams to fright thee after fate?   180
No ghost, no goblins, that still passage keep;
For all is there serene in that eternal sleep.

For all the dismal tales, that poets tell,
Are verified on earth, and not in hell.
No Tantalus looks up with fearful eye,   185
Or dreads th' impending rock to crush him from on high;
But fear of chance on earth disturbs our easy hours,
Or vain imagined wrath of vain imagined powers.
No Tityus* torn by vultures lies in hell;
Nor could the lobes of his rank liver swell   190
To that prodigious mass, for their eternal meal;
Not though his monstrous bulk had covered o'er
Nine spreading acres, or nine thousand more;
Not though the globe of earth had been the giant's floor;
Nor in eternal torments could he lie,   195
Nor could his corpse sufficient food supply
But he's the Tityus who, by love oppressed,
Or tyrant passion preying on his breast,
And ever anxious thoughts is robbed of rest,
The Sisyphus is he, whom noise and strife   200
Seduce from all the soft retreats of life,
To vex the government, disturb the laws;
Drunk with the fumes of popular applause,
He courts the giddy crowd to make him great,
And sweats and toils in vain, to mount the sovereign seat.   205
For, still to aim at power and still to fail,
Ever to strive, and never to prevail,
What is it, but, in reason's true account,
To heave the stone against the rising mount?
Which urged, and laboured, and forced up with pain,   210

---

*A Titan, son of Mother Earth, who tried to rape the goddess Leto, was slain by Zeus, and was sent to Hades, where his body reportedly covered nine acres.

Recoils, and rolls impetuous down, and smokes along the plain.
Then, still to treat thy ever-craving mind
With every blessing, and of every kind
Yet never fill thy ravening appetite,
Though years and seasons vary thy delight,   215
Yet nothing to be seen of all the store,
But still the wolf within thee barks for more;
This is the fable's moral, which they tell
Of fifty foolish virgins* damned in hell
To leaky vessels, which the liquor spill   220
To vessels of their sex, which none could ever fill.
As for the dog, the furies, and their snakes,
The gloomy caverns, and the burning lakes,
And all the vain infernal trumpery,
They neither are, nor were, nor e'er can be.   225
But here, in earth, the guilty have in view
The mighty pains to mighty mischiefs due;
Racks, prisons, poisons, the Tarpeian rock,†
Stripes, hangmen, pitch, and the suffocating smoke;

And last, and most, if these were cast behind,   230
The avenging horror of a conscious mind;
Whose deadly fear anticipates the blow,
And sees no end of punishment and woe,
But looks for more, at the last gasp of breath;
This makes a hell on earth and life a death.   235
Meantime, when thoughts of death disturb thy head,
Consider Ancus,‡ great and good, is dead;
Ancus, thy better far, was born to die.
And thou, dost thou bewail mortality?
So many monarchs with their mighty state,   240
Who ruled the world, were overruled by fate.
That haughty king,§ who lorded o'er the main,
And whose stupendous bridge did the wild waves restrain,
(In vain they foamed, in vain they threatened wreck,
While his proud legions marched upon their back)   245
Him death, a greater monarch, overcame;
Nor spared his guards the more, for their immortal name.

---

*The Danaids, who murdered their husbands.
†Cliff from which malefactors were hurled to their death in ancient Rome.
‡Legendary fourth king of Rome.
§Xerxes, king of Persia (590?–465 B.C.E.)

The Roman chief, the Carthaginian dread,
Scipio,* the thunderbolt of war, is dead,
And, like a common slave, by fate in triumph led.   250
The founders of invented art are lost;
And wits, who made eternity their boast.
Where now is Homer, who possessed the throne?
Th' immortal work remains, the immortal author's gone.
Democritus, perceiving age invade,   255
His body weakened, and his mind decayed,
Obeyed the summons with a cheerful face;
Made haste to welcome death, and met him half the race.
That stroke even Epicurus could not bar,
Though he in wit surpassed mankind, as far   260
As does the midday sun the midnight star,
And thou, dost thou disdain to yield thy breath,
Whose every life is little more than death?
More than one half by lazy sleep possessed;
And when awake, thy soul but nods at best,   265
Day-dreams and sickly thoughts revolving in thy breast.
Eternal troubles haunt thy anxious mind,
Whose cause and cure thou never hopest to find;
But still uncertain, with thyself at strife,
Thou wanderest in the labyrinth of life.   270
      O, if the foolish race of man, who find
A weight of cares still pressing on their mind,
Could find as well the cause of this unrest,
And all this burden lodged with the breast;
Sure they would change their course, nor live as now,   275
Uncertain what to wish, or what to vow.
Uneasy both in country and in town,
They search a place to lay their burden down.

One, restless in his palace, walks abroad,
And vainly thinks to leave behind the load,   280
But straight returns; for he's as restless there,
And finds there's no relief in open air.
Another to his villa would retire,
And spurs as hard as if it were on fire;
No sooner entered at his country door,   285

*Either Publius Cornelius Scipio Africanus Major (236?–183? B.C.E.)the elder, Roman general
who defeated Hannibal (202), or Publius Cornelius Scipio Aemilianus Africanus (185?–129 B.C.E.)
the younger, the general who destroyed Carthage (146)in the Third Punic War.

But he begins to stretch, and yawn, and snore.
Or seeks the city which he left before.
Thus every man o'erworks his weary will,
To shun himself, and to shake off his ill.
The shaking fit returns, and hangs upon him still.   290
No prospect of repose, nor hope of ease,
The wretch is ignorant of his disease;
Which, known, would all his fruitless trouble spare,
For he would know the worth of all his care:
Then would he search more deeply for the cause,   295
And study Nature well, and Nature's laws;
For in this moment lies not the debate,
But on the future, fixed, eternal state;
That never-changing state, which all must keep,
Whom death has doomed to everlasting sleep.   300
Why are we then so fond of mortal life,
Beset with dangers, and maintained with strife?
A life, which all our care can never save;
One fate attends us, and one common grave.

Besides, we tread but with a perpetual round;   305
We ne'er strike out, but beat the former ground,
And the same mawkish joys in the same track are found.
For still we think an absent blessing best,
Which cloys, and is no blessing when possessed;
A new arising wish expels it from the breast.   310
The feverish thirst of life increases still;
We call for more and more, and never have our fill;
Yet know not what tomorrow we shall try,
What dregs of life in the last draught may lie.
Nor, by the longest life we can attain,   315
One moment from the length of death we gain;
For all behind belongs to his eternal reign.
When once the fates have cut the mortal thread,
The man as much to all intents is dead,
Who dies today, and will as long be so,   320
As he who died a thousand years ago.

(trans. John Dryden)

CATULLUS (84–54 B.C.E.)

This passionate, brash, and sometimes brutal young poet created a theme of mortalist seduction that was destined to find thousands of imitators in the centuries that followed: give yourself to me now, the impatient literary wooer insists, because this world is all we have; or, as Andrew Marvell (d. 1678) puts it in "To His Coy Mistress," "Thy beauty shall no more be found; / Nor, in thy marble vault, shall sound / My echoing song; then worms shall try / That long-preserved virginity, / And your quaint honor turned to dust, / And into ashes all my lust: / The grave's a fine and private place, / But none, I think, do there embrace." Catullus' love affair with a married woman named Clodia, whom he called Lesbia, went badly awry; nonetheless it helped to launch what may be the most enduring topos in Western love poetry—a cliché that never seems to lose its bite.

CARMEN # 5

Dear *Lesbia*, let us love and play,
Not caring what Old Age can say;
The Sun does set, again does rise,
And with fresh Lustre gild the Skies.
When once extinguished is our Light,
We're wrapped in everlasting Night.
A thousand times my lips then kiss
An hundred more renew the bliss;
Another thousand add to these,
An hundred more will not suffice,
Another thousand will not do,
Another hundred are too few.
A thousand more these Joys we'll prove,
Till we're extravagant in Love,
Till no malicious Spy can guess
To what a wonderful Excess
My *Lesbia* and I did kiss.

(trans. John Chatwin [ca. 1685])

HORACE (65-8 B.C.E.)

The great Roman poet Quintus Horatius Flaccus (Horace) has a deserved reputation for being both exquisite and nearly untranslatable, but he is too distinguished a mortalist to ignore. In his *Epistles* (I.iv.15–16) he calls himself a "fat, sleek hog, with well-tended skin, from Epicurus' herd" (*me pinguem et nitidum bene curata cute . . . Epicuri de grege porcum*). He does rank as one of the supreme Epicureans in all of literature, but no one would ever think of this playful, elegant, mundane, yet earnest poet as porcine in any other way. Horace's famous injunction *carpe diem* sums up his balanced, humane mortalism.

ODES, I.11

Strive not, Leuconoë, to know what end
The gods above to me or thee will send;
Nor with astrologers consult at all,
That thou mayst better know what can befall:
Whether thou livest more winters, or thy last
Be this, which Tyrene waves 'gainst rocks do cast.
Be wise! Drink free, and in so short a space
Do not protracted hopes of life embrace:
Whilst we are talking, envious time doth slide;
This day's thine own; the next may be denied.

(trans. Thomas Hawkins)

II.14

Alas, dear friend, the fleeting years
    In everlasting circles run,
In vain you spend your vows and prayers,
    They roll, and ever will roll on.

Should hecatombs each rising morn
    On cruel Pluto's altar die,
Should costly loads of incense burn,
    Their fumes ascending to the sky;

You could not gain a moment's breath,
    Or move the haughty king below,
Nor would inexorable death
    Defer an hour the fatal blow.
In vain we shun the din of war,
    And terrors of the stormy main,
In vain with anxious breasts we fear
    Unwholesome Sirius' sultry reign;

We all must view the Stygian flood
    That silent cuts the dreary plains,
And cruel Danaus' bloody brood
    Condemned to everduring pains.

Your shady groves, your pleasing wife,
    And fruitful fields, my dearest friend,
You'll leave together with your life:
    Alone the cypress shall attend.

After your death, the lavish heir
    Will quickly drive away his woe;
The wine you kept with so much care
    Along the marble floor shall flow.

                 (trans. Samuel Johnson)

from III.29

VII

Enjoy the present smiling hour,
    And put it out of Fortune's power;
The tide of business, like the running stream,
    Is sometimes high, and sometimes low,
A quiet ebb, or a tempestuous flow,
    And always in extreme.

Now with a noiseless gentle course
It keeps within the middle bed;
Anon it lifts aloft the head,
And bears down all before it with impetuous force:
And trunks of trees come rolling down
Sheep and their folds together drown;
Both house and homestead into seas are borne,
And rocks from their old foundations torn,
And woods, made thin with winds, their scattered honours mourn.

VIII

Happy the man, and happy he alone,
He, who can still call today his own:
He, who secure within, can say
"Tomorrow do thy worst, for I have lived today.
Be fair or foul, or rain, or shine,
The joys I have possessed, in spite of fate, are mine.
Not Heav'n itself upon the past has power;
But what has been, has been, and I have had my hour."

(trans. John Dryden)

IV.7

The snows are fled away, leaves on the shaws*
And grasses in the mead renew their birth,
The river to the river-bed withdraws,
And altered is the fashion of the earth,
The Nymphs and Graces three put off their fear
And unapparelled in the woodland play.
The swift hour and the brief prime of the year
Say to the soul, *Thou wast not born for aye.*
Thaw follows frost; hard on the heel of spring
Treads summer sure to die, for hard on hers
Comes autumn, with his apples scattering;
Then back to wintertide, when nothing stirs.
But oh, whate'er the sky-led seasons mar,
Moon upon moon rebuilds it with her beams;

---

*small woods

Come we where Tullus* and where Ancus are
　　And good Aeneas, we are dust and dreams.
Torquatus,† if the gods in heaven shall add
　　The morrow to the day, what tongue hath told?
Feast then thy heart, for what thy heart has had
　　The finger of no heir will ever hold,
When thou descendest once the shades among,
　　The stern assize and equal judgment o'er,
Not thy long lineage nor thy golden tongue,
　　No, not thy righteousness, shall friend thee more.
Night holds Hippolytus‡ the pure of stain,
　　Diana steads him nothing, he must stay;
And Theseus leaves Pirithous§ in the chain
　　The love of comrades cannot take away.

　　　　　　　　　　　　　　(trans. A. E. Housman)

---

*The third king of Rome.
†The addressee of the poem, a friend of Horace.
‡Son of Theseus, king of Athens, innocently destroyed by his father's curse.
§Close friends; when Pirithous died and descended to Hades, Theseus tried but failed to bring him back.

SENECA (LUCIUS ANNAEUS SENECA, "THE YOUNGER," 4? B.C.E.—65 C.E.)

O nce celebrated as a stylist and moral philosopher, Seneca has fallen out of favor with modern readers, whom he often strikes as fussy and self-impor-tant. He was also a playwright, and in the following chorus from his *Troades* (The Trojan Women) he made one of the most trenchant summaries ever of the mortalist position. Ironically, the translator of this passage, John Wilmot, Earl of Rochester (1647–1680) was notorious during his brief, tumultuous life as a god-less hedonist, but reportedly became an earnest Christian on his deathbed.

FROM *TROADES*

After death nothing is, and nothing death:
The utmost limit of a gasp of breath.
Let the ambitious zealot lay aside
His hopes of heaven: whose faith is but his pride.
Let slavish souls lay by their fear,
Nor be concerned which way or where
After this life they shall be hurled:
Dead, we become the lumber of the world.
And to that mass of matter shall be swept
Where things destroyed with things unborn are kept:
Devouring time swallows us whole,
Impartial death confounds body and soul.
For Hell, and the foul Fiend that rules
The everlasting fiery gaols,
Devised by rogues, dreaded by fools,
With his grim grisly dog that keeps the door,
Are senseless stories, idle tales,
Dreams, whimsies, and no more.

(trans. John Wilmot, Earl of Rochester)

HADRIAN (76–138 C.E.)

Almost the shortest and perhaps the most endearing bit of mortalist poetry comes from the pen of the Roman emperor Hadrian, five lines that he reportedly composed on his deathbed. It has been translated, unsuccessfully, time and time again. For the record, the Latin text follows:

> animula vagula blandula,
> hospes comesque corporis,
> quae nunc abibis in loca,
> pallida, rigida, nudula,
> nec ut soles dabis iocos?

> (Little soul, little wandering soul, little endearing soul /
> the guest and companion of the body / what places will you
> go to now? / pale, stiff, naked little soul / nor will you
> crack jokes as you are wont to do.)

John Donne captured the first two lines ("My little wandring sportful Soul, / Guest and companion of my body"), but he left off there; the most popular version has been that of Lord Byron (another fervent mortalist):

> Ah! Gentle, fleeting, wav'ring sprite,
> Friend and associate of this clay!
> To what unknown region borne,
> Wilt thou, now, wing thy distant flight?
> No more, with wonted humour gay,
> But pallid, cheerless, and forlorn.

(1806)

MARCUS AURELIUS
(120–181 C.E.)

The great Stoic emperor, Marcus Aurelius, who kept a notebook in intense, crabbed Greek, known as his *Meditations* (though originally entitled *To Himself*), was technically an agnostic about the fate of the soul after death: perhaps it perished, perhaps it survived in some sort of fusion with the universe. But much of what he says is perfectly consistent with mortalism; and his frequent admonitions not to fear death but to prepare for it as something natural and proper suggest that he felt more anxiety about it than he openly acknowledges.

FROM *MEDITATIONS*

II.17

Of the life of man the duration is but a point, its substance streaming away, its perception dim, the fabric of the entire body prone to decay, and the soul a vortex, and fortune incalculable, and fame uncertain. In a word all things of the body are as a river, and the things of the soul as a dream and a vapor; and life is a warfare and a pilgrim's sojourn, and fame after death is only forgetfulness, What then is it that can help us on our way? One thing and one thing alone—Philosophy; . . . [The philosopher should above all wait] for death with a good grace as being but a setting free of the elements of which every thing living is made up. But if there be nothing terrible in each thing being continuously changed into another thing, why should a man look askance at the change and dissolution of all things. For it is but the way of Nature, and in the way of nature there can be no evil.

IV.41

Thou art a *little soul bearing up a corpse*, as Epictetus said.

IV.48

Cease not to bear in mind how many physicians are dead after puckering up their brows so often over their patients; and how many astrologers after making a great parade of predicting the death of others; and how many philosophers after endless disquisitions on death and immortality, how many great captains after butchering thousands; how many tyrants, after exercising with revolting insolence their power of life and death, as though themselves immortal; and how many entire cities are, if I may use the expression, dead, Helice and Pompeii and Herculaneuum, and other without number.

Turn also to all, one after another, that come within thine own knowledge, One closed a friend's eyes and was then himself laid out, and the friend who closed his, he too was laid out—and all this in a few short years. In a word, fail not to note how short-lived are all mortal things, and how paltry—yesterday a little mucus [i.e., semen], to-morrow a mummy or burnt ash. Pass then through this tiny span of time in accordance with nature, and come to thy journey's end with a good grace, just as an olive falls when it is fully ripe, praising the earth that bare it and grateful to the tree that gave it growth.

V.23

Think often on the swiftness with which the things that exist and that are coming into existence are swept past us and carried out of sight. For all substance is as a river in ceaseless flow, its activities ever changing and its causes subject to countless variations, and scarcely anything stable; and ever beside us is this infinity of the past and yawning abyss of the future, wherein all things are disappearing. Is he not senseless who in such an environment puffs himself up, or is distracted, or frets as over a trouble lasting and far-reaching?

VI.28

Death is a release from the impressions of the sense, and from impulses that make us their puppets, from the vagaries of the mind, and the hard service of the flesh.

VI.36

Asia, Europe, corners of the Universe: the whole Ocean a drop of the Universe: Athos but a little clod therein: all the present a point in Eternity:—everything on a tiny scale, so easily changed, so quickly vanished.

VII.21

A little while and thou wilt have forgotten everything, a little while and everything will have forgotten thee.

VIII.18

That which dies is not cast out of the Universe. As it remains here, it also suffers change here and is dissolved into its own constituents, which are the elements of the Universe and thy own. Yes, and they too suffer change and murmur not.

VIII.31

The court of Augustus—wife, daughter, descendants, ancestors, sister, Agrippa, kinsfolk, household, friends, Areius [Augustus' personal philosopher], Maecenas, physicians, diviners—dead, the whole court of them! Pass on then to other records and the death not of individuals but of a clan, as of the Pompeii. And that well-known epitaph, *Last of his race*—think over it and the anxiety shown by the man's ancestors that they might leave a successor. But after all some one must be the last of the line—here again the death of a whole race!

VIII.37

Does Pantheia [the mistress of Verus, co-emperor of Marcus] now watch by the urn of her lord or Pergamus [his freedman]? What, does Chabrias or Diotimus by Hadrian's? Absurd! What then? Had they sat there till now, would the dead have been aware of it? And, if aware of it, would they have been pleased? And, if pleased, would that have made the mourners immortal? Was it not destined that these like others should become old women and old men and then die? What then, when they were dead, would be left for those whom they had mourned to do? It is all stench and corruption in a sack of skin.

IX.28

Presently the earth will cover us all. It too will anon be changed. And the resulting product will go on from change to change, and so for ever and ever. When a man thinks of these successive waves of change and transformation, and their rapidity, he will hold every mortal thing in scorn.

IX.30

Take a bird's-eye view of the world, its endless gatherings and endless ceremonials, voyagings manifold in storm and calm, and the vicissitudes of things coming into being, participating in being, ceasing to be. Reflect too on the life lived long ago by other men, and the life that shall be lived after thee, and is now being lived in barbarous countries; and how many have never even heard thy name, and how many will very soon forget it. And how many who now perhaps acclaim, will very soon blame thee, and that neither memory nor fame nor anything else whatever is worth reckoning.

IX.33

All that thine eyes behold will soon perish and they, who live to see it perish, will in their turn perish no less quickly; and he who outlives all his contemporaries and he who dies before his time will be as one in the grave.

IX.36

Seeds of decay in the underlying material of everything—water, dust, bones, reek! Again, marble but nodules of earth, and gold and silver but dross, garments merely hair-tufts, and purple only blood. And so with everything else. The soul too another like thing and liable to change from this to that.

XII.36

Man, thou hast been a citizen in this World-City, what matters it to thee for five years or a hundred? For under its laws equal treatment is meted out to all. What hardship then is there in being banished from the city, not by a tyrant or an unjust judge but by Nature who settled thee in it? So might a praetor who commissions a comic actor, dismiss him from the stage. *But I have not played my five acts, but only three.* Very possibly, but in life three acts count as a full play. For he, that is responsible for thy composition originally and thy dissolution now, decides when it is complete. But thou art responsible for neither. Depart then with a good grace, for he also that dismisses thee is gracious.

(trans. C. R. Haines [1916])

BEDE THE VENERABLE
(673?–735 C.E.)

Occasional flashes of mortalism appear throughout medieval works of Christian edification, such as the *Ecclesiastical History of England* by the Anglo-Saxon monk Bede the Venerable. In the following excerpt, during a discussion at the court of King Edwin (ca. 627) about whether to accept Christianity, an unnamed nobleman argues that the new religion might be a good thing, given the harsh realities of life without otherworldly consolations.

FROM THE *ECCLESIASTICAL HISTORY OF ENGLAND*

"My king," he said, "this is what the life of human beings on earth here and now seems to me, with regard to the uncertain amount of time allotted to us: it is as if, while you were sitting down to table with your captains and servants, when the days are shortest and a fire is lit in the middle of the dining hall, warming up the room, while the rain storms or blizzards are raging everywhere outside; and as if a sparrow should fly up to the house and flit through it like a shot, coming in one window and a moment later leaving by another: for as long as the bird is inside, it does not feel the wintry storm, but once it has finished its tiny, momentary course through light and warmth, it flies back, out of the winter night into the winter night, and is swept away from your eyes. Thus, the life of men appears for an instant, but whatever follows it, and whatever went before—of that we have no idea at all."

(trans. Peter Heinegg)

MICHEL DE MONTAIGNE
(1533–1592)

B orn and raised a Catholic (though his mother was of Portuguese Jewish stock) Montaigne was the most nominal of believers. Ever the Pyrrhonist (skeptic) and Epicurean, he found his moral and philosophical models in classical antiquity, as we see in this early essay on death, where he draws upon Lucretius and Horace in particular to encourage the reader (and himself) to take a sober and serene view of death. In some ways Montaigne is doing little more than rehearsing commonplaces, but he does so with his usual vigorous and unaffected eloquence. Despite the brief (and puzzling) reference to "Holy Scripture" in the first paragraph, there is every indication that Montaigne takes the truth of mortalism for granted.

ESSAYS I.20, "THAT TO PHILOSOPHIZE IS TO LEARN TO DIE"

Cicero says that to philosophize is nothing but preparing for death. That's because study and contemplation in a sense draw our soul out of us and occupy it apart from the body, which is a kind of apprenticeship for, and resemblance of, death. Or else it's because all the wisdom and discourse of the world ultimately comes down to this point: to teach us to have no fear of death. To tell the truth, either reason is a joke or it has to aim purely at our contentment, and all its efforts have to tend toward making us live well and at our ease, as Holy Scripture says. All the opinions of the world agree on this: pleasure is our goal—though they take different ways to get there. Otherwise people would dismiss them at once. Who would listen to anyone who would make his goal our pain and discomfort?

The disagreements of the philosophic sects on this point are just quibbles. *Let's quickly pass over such subtle nonsense* [Seneca]. There's more pigheadedness and idle jabbing than suits such a sacred profession. But whatever role a man takes on, he's always playing his own among them. People can say what they like, in virtue itself the ultimate goal we have in view is sensual pleasure. I like to beat them over the ears with that word, which so rubs them the wrong way. And if it means some sort of supreme pleasure and extreme satisfaction, that's due more to help from virtue than from any other source. The fact that this voluptuousness is more hearty, sinewy, robust, and virile only makes it that much more seriously voluptuous. And we ought to have given it the name of pleasure, which is more favorable, more sweet and natural, not that of vigor. . . .

Now among the principal benefits of virtue is contempt for death, a device that supplies our life with a soft tranquility and gives us a pure and pleasant taste of it, without which all other sensual pleasure is wiped out. That is why all the rules concur and agree on this point. And though they unanimously lead us as well to hold in contempt pain, poverty, and the other accidents to which human life is subject, they don't all go to the same trouble, both because these accidents are not equally necessary (most men pass through life without tasting poverty, while others do so without suffering from pain and illness, like Xenophilus the musician, who lived a hundred and six years in perfect health), and partly because if worse comes to worst, death can put a stop to it, whenever we please, and cut off all other troubles. But as for death, it is inevitable. . . .

The goal of our career is death. It is the necessary object that we all have in view. If it terrifies us, how can we take a step forward without running a fever? The remedy of the rabble is not to think about it. But how can we let brutal stupidity give rise to such gross blindness! . . .

What difference does it make, you'll tell me, how it comes about, so long you don't trouble yourself about it? I agree; and however we can take shelter from blows, even under a calf's skin, I'm not one to shrink from it. It's enough for me to pass my time in comfort; and I'll take the best game I can get, though in other ways it may be as inglorious and unedifying as you like. . . .

But it is madness to think one can get there that way. They go, they come, they trot, they dance—no word of death. That's fine, but when it comes, either to them or to their wives, children, and friends, catching them by surprise and defenseless, what torments, what cries, what rage, what despair overwhelms them? Did you ever see anything so downcast, so changed, so confounded? We have to make provisions for this sooner; and this beastlike indifference, even if it had any place in the mind of a thoughtful person—which I find completely impossible—charges too much for its merchandise. If it were an enemy that could be avoided, I'd advise borrowing the coward's weapons. But since that can't be done, since it will catch you fleeing like a poltroon or facing it bravely . . .—let's learn to bear up firmly under its assault and to fight it. And to begin to rob it of its greatest advantage against us, let's take an approach totally different from the usual one. Let's rid it of its strangeness, let's practice it, let's get used to it. Let's have nothing in our thoughts as often as death. At every moment let's picture it to our imagination in all its guises. When a horse stumbles, when a tile falls off a roof, at a tiny pinprick, let's instantly chew this over: "Well, suppose that were death itself?" And on that point let's stiffen ourselves and make a serious effort. Amid feasts and merrymaking let's always sing the same refrain, to remember our condition and never let ourselves get so carried away by pleasure that we don't from time to time recall in how many ways this joy of ours is a prey to death, and how many holds death threaten us with. That's what the Egyptians did when in the middle of their feasts and while tasting their finest fare, they had a skeleton carried in as a reminder to their guests. . . .

It's uncertain where death is waiting for us; let's wait for it everywhere. Premeditation of death is premeditation of freedom. Those who have learned how to die have unlearned how to be a slave, Knowing how to die sets us free from all subjection and constraint. There is nothing evil in life for those who have clearly realized that being deprived of life is not an evil. When the wretched king of Macedon sent a man to Aemilius Paulus, who held him prisoner, to beg him not to lead him in his triumph, the Roman replied: "Let him ask himself!"

In truth, in all things, unless nature lends some help, it's hard for art and industriousness to make much headway. By nature I'm not melancholic, but dreamy. All my life there's nothing I've spent more time imagining than death. Even in the most licentious season . . . amid ladies and games, someone would think I was all caught up in chewing over some jealous thought or some uncertain hope, while I was actually brooding about someone or other who had been ambushed a few days before by a hot fever and by death, as he was leaving a feast like this one, his head full of idleness, love, and good times—just like me. . . .

I didn't wrinkle my forehead over that thought any more than over another. It's impossible, at first, not to feel the sting of such thoughts. But by picking them up and going back over them, in the long run there's no doubt they can be tamed. Otherwise, speaking for myself, I would be in continual fright and frenzy; for nobody ever so distrusted his life, nobody ever counted less on his survival. Health, which up till now I have enjoyed—it's been very vigorous and rarely interrupted—doesn't lengthen my hope of life, and illnesses don't cut it short. Every minute it seems to me that I'm stealing away. And I keep humming to myself: "Whatever can be done some other day can be done today." In fact, risks and dangers don't bring us any closer our end—or not much; and if we think, putting aside the accident that seems most threatening, how many million other ones remain hanging over our heads, we'll find that whether sprightly or feverish, out at sea or safe at home, in battle or at rest, death is equally close. . . .

Someone paging through my notebooks the other day found a memorandum about something I wanted done after my death. I told him—and it was true—that although I was only a league away from my house, and though lusty and well, I had hastened to write it down right there, as I could never be sure I'd get home. As a person who is constantly brooding over my thoughts and embedding them within me, I'm at all times about as ready as I can be. And the coming of death will be no news to me. . . .

People will say that the facts of death so far surpass the image that the best fencer in the world will lose when he comes to it. Let them talk; premeditation doubtless gives a grand advantage. And there's more: nature itself lends a hand

and encourages us. And then, is it nothing to go at least that far without losing composure and running a fever? If death comes quickly and violently, we don't have the leisure to fear it; if it comes differently, I notice that as I get caught up in the disease, I naturally acquire a certain disdain for life. I find that I have a much harder time digesting my resolution to die when I'm healthy than when I'm feverish. Insofar as I no longer cling so firmly to the comforts of life, the less I can use and enjoy them, I look on death with a much less frightened eye. This makes me hope that the farther I get from life and the closer I come to death, the more easily I'll come to terms with the exchange. . . .

Caesar once had a soldier of his guard, a worn-out, broken-down man, come up to him in the street to ask permission to kill himself. Seeing his decrepit condition, Caesar replied with a laugh: "So you think you're alive, do you?" If one were to fall into such a state all of a sudden, I don't think we could endure the change. But, led by nature's hand down a gentle and almost unnoticeable slope, little by little, one step at a time, she rolls us into that wretched state and gets us used to it; so that we feel no shock when youth dies within us, which is really and truly a harder death than the total death of a languishing life or death from old age. The leap from being badly off to not being at all is not such a jolt as it is from a sweet and flourishing state to one that is hard and painful. . . .

What does it matter when it comes, since it's inevitable? When a man who told Socrates, "The thirty tyrants have condemned you to death," he replied: "And nature has condemned them."

How stupid to trouble ourselves about passing over to where we'll be free of all trouble!

As our birth brought us the birth of all things, our death will bring us the death of all things. So it's equally foolish to weep because we won't be alive a hundred years from now as it is to weep because we weren't alive a hundred years ago. . . .

Nothing offers grounds for complaint that comes only once. Does it make sense to fear for so long a thing that is so short? Living a long time or a short time—it's made all one by death, because "long" and "short" don't apply to things that don't exist anymore. Aristotle says that there are little animals by the river Hypanis that live only a day. The one that dies at eight o'clock in the morning dies in its youth; the one that dies at five in the afternoon dies in its decrepitude. Which one of us wouldn't laugh to see this tiny bit of duration rated as happy or unhappy? All talk of our long or short duration, if we compare it with eternity, or even with the duration of mountains, rivers, stars, trees, and even some animals, is no less ridiculous.

But Nature forces us to it. "Leave this world," she says, "as you entered it. The same passage that you made from death to life, without passion or fear, make it again from life to death. Your death is a piece of the order of the universe, it's a piece of the life of the world. . . .

"Am I supposed to change for your sake this beautiful arrangement of things? Death is the condition of your creation, it is a part of you; you're fleeing from your selves. This being of yours which you enjoy is equally divided between death and life. The first day of your birth sends you on your way to die as it does to live. . . .

"Everything that you give to life you steal from life; life lives at its own expense. The constant work of your life is building up death. You're in death while you're in life; for you're after death when you're no longer in life.

"Or, if you want to put it this way, you're dead after life; but during life you're dying; and death strikes the dying much more roughly than the dead, and more sharply and essentially.

"If you've profited from your life, you've had your fill of it; go off in satisfaction. . . . If you haven't known how to use it, if it was no good to you, why do you care that you've lost it, what do you want more of it for? Life in itself is neither good nor evil: it's a place of good and evil depending on how much room you've given either of them.

"And if you've lived a day, you've seen everything. One day is equal to all days. There's no other light, no other night. This sun, this noon, these stars, this cosmos is the very same one that your ancestors enjoyed and that will entertain your great-nephew. . . . And at the worst, the distribution and variety of all the acts of my comedy is completed in a year. If you've noted the swing and sway of my four seasons, they embrace the infancy, the youth, the manhood, and the old age of the world. It's played its part; it knows no other trick except to start over. It'll always be the same. . . .

"Make room for others, as others have for you.

"Equality is the most important part of equity. Who can complain of being included where everyone is included? So, live as long as you like, you won't cut back on the time you'll have to be dead; it's all for naught; you'll spend just as much time in the condition that you fear, as if you'd died in your cradle. . . .

"Death is no more to be feared than nothing, if there was anything less than nothing . . . It doesn't concern you dead or alive: alive, because you exist; dead, because you no longer exist.

"No one dies before his time. The time you leave behind was no more yours than the time that passed before your birth, and it's no more of your business. . . .

"Wherever your life ends, it's all there. The usefulness of living is not how much you stretch it out, but how you use it: some people have lived a long, but lived little; pay attention to it while you're in it. Your will decides, not the number of years, where you have lived enough. Did you think you would never get to where you never stopped going? There has never yet been a road without an end.

"And if company can give you solace, isn't the world keeping in step with you? . . .

"Doesn't everything swing along as you do? Is there anything that doesn't grow old just as you do? A thousand human beings, a thousand animals, and a thousand other creatures are dying at the very same instant when you die. . . .

"Why do you shrink from it if you can't go backwards? You have seen enough people who were lucky to die, thereby escaping great misery. Have you seen anyone who was the worse for dying? What utter simplemindedness to condemn a thing that you haven't experienced, either in person or by anyone else. Why do you complain about me and about destiny? Are we doing you wrong? Is it for you to govern us, or for us to govern you? Though your age is not yet completed, your life is. A little man is a whole man, as is a big man. Neither humans nor their lives are measured by the ell.

"Chiron refused immortality when he was told about its conditions by the very god of time and duration, his father Saturn. Imagine truly how an everlasting life would be so much less bearable and so much more painful than the life I've given you. If you didn't have death, you would curse me unceasingly for having deprived you of it. I've deliberately mixed in with it a little bitterness to prevent you, having seen all its comforts, from embracing it too eagerly and indiscreetly. To place you in that middle condition I ask you to accept, where one neither flees life nor refuses death, I've tempered both of them with sweetness and bitterness.

"I taught Thales, the first of your sages, that living and dying were indifferent; and so, when a man asked him why he didn't just die, he replied very wisely: 'Because it doesn't make any difference.'

"Water, earth, air, fire, and the other parts of this system of mine are no more instruments of your life than instruments of your death. Why do you fear your last day? It adds no more to your death than each of the others. The last step doesn't create your weariness, it manifests it. All days are headed toward death, the last one gets there."

Such is the good advice of our mother nature. Now I've often pondered how it happens that in wars the face of death, whether we see it in ourselves or others, strikes us as incomparably less terrifying than in our houses (otherwise armies would be made up of doctors and crybabies) and, since death is always one and the same, why do you still see far more confidence in facing it among villagers and the lower orders than among other people? In truth, I think it's those terrifying looks and preparations with which we surround it that frighten us more than death: a whole new way of living; the cries of mothers, wives, and children; the visits from people stunned and paralyzed with grief; the presence of all the pale and weeping servants; a dark room; lighted candles; our bedside besieged by doctors and preachers; in a word, nothing but horror and dread around us. There we are, already laid-out and buried. Children are even afraid of their friends when they see wearing masks, and so we're afraid of ours. We have to tear away the mask from things as well as from persons; once it's off, all we'll find beneath it is the same death that a valet or simple chambermaid went through not long ago without fear. Happy the death that has no leisure for preparing such a song and dance.

(trans. Peter Heinegg)

CHIDIOCK TICHBORNE
(D. 1586)

Tichborne was an aristocratic conspirator against Queen Elizabeth. Arrested and condemned to be hanged and disemboweled, on the eve of his death he wrote this poem, which illustrates Dr. Johnson's famous dictum: "When a man knows he is to be hanged in a fortnight, it concentrates his mind wonderfully." Although a Catholic, Tichborne pointedly makes no reference to another and better world.

TICHBORNE'S ELEGY

My prime of youth is but a frost of cares,
My feast of joy is but a dish of pain,
My crop of corn is but a field of tares,
And all my good is but vain hope of gain;
The day is past, and yet I saw no sun,
And now I live, and now my life is done.

My tale was heard and yet it was not told,
My fruit is fallen and yet my leaves are green,
My youth is spent and yet I am not old,
I saw the world and yet I was not seen;
My thread is cut and yet it is not spun,
And now I live, and now my life is done.

I sought my death and found it in my womb,
I looked for life and saw it was a shade,
I trod the earth and knew it was my tomb,
And now I die, and now I was but made;
My glass is full, and now my glass is run,
And now I live, and now my life is done.

WILLIAM SHAKESPEARE
(1564–1616)

In a broad sense one could quote practically all the plays and poems of Shake-speare as a meditation on mortalism, but one of the most powerful, and end-lessly cited, instances of it would have to be the first scene of Act V of *Hamlet*, which takes place in the cemetery where Ophelia is about to be buried. Hamlet's confrontation with the skull of Yorick brings him to the lowest point of his reflec-tions on the triumph of death—a reality that he winds up accepting but not tran-scending. The final scene of *King Lear* shows us mortalism at its most desolating. Here, as in all tragedy, from Aeschylus to Shakespeare and beyond, the suffering of the protagonists and the whole meaning of the play become empty unless death is understood as completely final. A postlude in some "better world," Christian or otherwise, is unthinkable here.

HAMLET, V.i.181–218

Hamlet. How long will a man lie i' the earth ere he rot?

Clown. Faith, if 'a be not rotten before 'a die (as we have many pocky corses nowadays that will scarce hold the laying in), 'a will last you some eight year or nine year. A tanner will last you nine year.

Hamlet. Why he, more than another?

Clown. Why, sir, his hide is so tanned with his trade that 'a will keep out water a great while, and your water is a great decayer of your whoreson dead body. Here's a skull that hath lien you i' th'earth three and twenty years.

Clown. A whoreson mad fellow's t was. Whose do you think it was?

Hamlet. Nay, I know not.

Clown. A pestilence on him for a mad rogue! 'A poured a flagon of Rhenish on my head once. This same skull, sir, was, sir, Yorick's skull, the King's jester.

Hamlet. This?

Clown. E'en that.

Hamlet. Let me see. [*Takes the skull.*] Alas, poor Yorick! I knew him, Horatio, a fellow of infinite jest, of most excellent fancy. He hath borne me on his back a thousand times. And now how abhorred in my imagination it is! My gorge rises at it. Here hung those lips that I have kissed I know not how oft. Where be your jibes now? Your gambols, your songs, your flashesof merriment that were wont to set the table on a roar? Not one to mock your own grinning? Quite chapfall'n? Now get you to my lady's chamber, and tell her, let her paint an inch thick, to this favor she must come. Make her laugh at that. Prithee, Horatio, tell me one thing.

Horatio. What's that, my lord.

Hamlet. Dost thou think Alexander looked o' this fashion i' th' earth?

Horatio. E'en so.

Hamlet. And smelt so? Pah! [*Puts down the skull.*]

Horatio. E'en so, my lord.

Hamlet. To what base uses we may return, Horatio! Why may not imagination trace the noble dust of Alexander till 'a find it stopping a bunghole?

Horatio. 'Twere to consider too curiously, to consider so.

Hamlet. No, faith, not a jot, but to follow him thither with modesty enough, and likelihood to lead it; as thus: Alexander died, Alexander was buried, Alexander returneth to dust; the dust is earth; of earth we make loam; and why of that loam whereto he was converted might they not stop a beer barrel?

Imperious Caesar, dead and turned to clay,
Might stop a hole to keep the wind away.
O that that earth which kept the world in awe
Should patch a wall t'expel the winter's flaw!

KING LEAR, ACT V, III, 259–319

[Enter Lear, with Cordelia in his arms [Gentleman, and others following]

Lear. Howl, howl, howl, howl! O, you are men of stone:
    Had I your tongues and eyes, I'd use them so

That heaven's vault should crack. She's gone for ever.
I know when one is dead and when one lives;
She's dead as earth. Lend me a looking-glass;
If that her breath will mist or stain the stone,
Why, then she lives.

Kent. Is this the promised end?

Edgar. Or image of that horror.

Albany. Fall and cease.

Lear. This feather stirs, she lives. If it be so,
It is a chance which does redeem all sorrows
That ever I have felt.

Kent. O my good master.

Lear. Prithee, away.

Edgar. 'Tis noble Kent, your friend.

Lear. A plague upon you, murderers, traitors all!
    I might have saved her; now she's gone for ever.
    Cordelia, Cordelia, stay a little. Ha,
    What is 't thou say'st? Her voice was ever soft,
    Gentle and low, an excellent thing in woman.
    I killed the slave that was a-hanging thee.

Gentleman. 'Tis true, my lords, he did.

Lear. Did I not, fellow?
    I have seen the day, with my good biting falchion
    I would have made them skip. I am old now,
    And these same crosses spoil me. Who are you?
    Mine eyes are not o' th' best: I'll tell you straight.

Kent. If Fortune brag of two she loved and hated,
    One of them we behold.

Lear. This is a dull sight. Are you not Kent?

Kent. The same,
    Your servant, Kent. Where is your servant Caius?

Lear. He's a good fellow, I can tell you that;
    And quickly too: he's dead and rotten.

Kent. No, my good lord; I am the very man.

Lear. I'll see that straight.

Kent. That from the first of difference and decay
Have followed your sad steps.

Lear. You are welcome hither.

Kent. Nor no man else: all's cheerless, dark and deadly.
Your eldest daughters have fordone themselves,
And desperately are dead.

Lear. Ay, so I think.

Albany. He knows not what he says, and vain is it
That we present ourselves to him.

Edgar. Very bootless.

Enter a Messenger.

Messenger. Edmund is dead, my lord.

Albany. That's but a trifle here.
You lords and noble friends, know our intent.
What comfort to this great decay may come
Shall be applied. For us, we will resign
During the life of this old majesty,
To him our absolute power: [*To Edgar and Kent)*
        you, to your rights;
With boot, and such addition as your honors
Have more than merited. All friends shall taste
The wages of their virtue, and all foes
The cup of their deservings. O, see, see!

Lear. And my poor fool is hanged: no, no, no life?
Why should a dog, a horse, a rat have life,
And thou no breath at all? Thou'lt come no more.
Never, never, never, never, never.
Pray you, undo this button. Thank you, sir.
Do you see this? Look on her. Look, her lips,
Look there, look there.

He dies.

Edgar. He faints. My lord, my lord!

Kent. Break, heart; I prithee, break.

Edgar. Look up, my lord.

Kent. Vex not his ghost: O, let him pass! He hates him
That would upon the rack of this tough world
Stretch him out longer.

Edgar. He is gone indeed.

Kent. The wonder is he hath endured so long:
He but usurped his life.

Albany. Bear them from hence. Our present business
Is general woe.

BLAISE PASCAL (1623–1662)

Apart from his fame as a mathematician and physicist, Pascal is best known as a brilliant Christian layman and a philosophical defender of the faith. But in his *Pensées* he sometimes speaks in the character of the *libertin*, the troubled unbeliever, for whom, did he but know it, Christianity offers the only way out of a dead-end world; and in this role Pascal's voice often takes on such haunting conviction that we can only wonder to what extent the *libertin* was echoing the dark and doubtful side of Pascal's own mind.

---

from *Pensées*

88. When I consider the brief duration of my life, swallowed up in the eternity that precedes and that follows it, the tiny space that I fill and even the space that I can see, overwhelmed in the infinite immensity of the spaces that I know not and that know nothing of me, I am terrified and astonished to see myself here rather than there; because there is no reason whatsoever why I should be here rather than there, and why now rather than then. Who has put me here? By whose order and guidance has this place and this time been assigned to me? *Memoria hospitis unius diei praetereuntis* [the memory of a guest who stays but a passing day].

227. The last act is bloody, however fine the comedy may be otherwise. In the end they throw dirt on your head, and that's it for ever.

264. Man is nothing but a reed, the weakest one in nature; but he's a thinking reed. The whole universe need not take arms to crush him; a vapor, a drop of water is enough to kill him. But even if the universe should crush him, man would still be nobler than what kills, because he knows that he dies, and as for the advantage that the universe has over him, the universe knows nothing of it.

91. The eternal silence of these infinite spaces fills me with terror.

355. [The voice of the unbeliever] "I don't know who put me in this world, nor what the world is nor what I myself am. I'm in a terrible state of ignorance about

everything. I don't know what my body is, nor my senses, nor my soul, nor that part of myself that thinks what I say, that reflects on everything and on itself, and that doesn't know itself any more than the rest. I see those terrifying spaces of the universe that lock me in, and I find myself attached to a corner of that vast expanse, without knowing why I am placed in this spot instead of another, nor why this bit of time given me to live has been assigned at this point instead of another, of all the eternity that has preceded me and that will follow me. I see nothing but infinities on all sides, which shut me in like an atom and like a shadow lasting just an instant that will not return. All that I know is that I must die soon, but what I know least of all is that very death that I'll never be able to avoid."

434. Imagine a number of men in chains, and all of them condemned to death, with some getting their throats cut in full sight of the others. Those who remain see their own condition in that of their fellows; and, looking at one another in pain and without hope, they wait their turn. This is a picture of the human condition.

(trans. Peter Heinegg)

DAVID HUME (1711–1776)

David Hume, the Scottish philosopher and historian, is probably the ablest champion of mortalism in modern times. With his clear, serene, understated prose Hume presents a devastating case against the survival of the soul, or any sort of personal identity, after death.

FROM *A TREATISE OF HUMAN NATURE*, BOOK I: OF THE UNDERSTANDING, SECTION VI, OF PERSONAL IDENTITY

There are some philosophers, who imagine we are every moment intimately conscious of what we call our SELF; that we feel its existence and its continuance in existence; and are certain, beyond the evidence of a demonstration, both of its perfect identity and simplicity. The strongest sensation, the most violent passion, say they, instead of distracting us from this view, only fix it the more intensely, and make us consider their influence on *self* either by their pain or pleasure. To attempt a farther proof of this were to weaken its evidence; since no proof can be deriv'd from any fact, of which we are so intimately conscious; nor is there anything, of which we can be certain, if we doubt of this.

Unluckily all these positive assertions are contrary to that very experience, which is pleaded for them, nor have we any idea of *self*, after the manner it is here explain'd. For from what impression cou'd this be deriv'd? This question 'tis impossible to answer without a manifest contradiction and absurdity; and yet 'tis a question, which must necessarily be answer'd, if we wou'd have the idea of self pass for clear and intelligible. It must be some one impression, that gives rise to every real idea. But self or person is not any one impression, but that to which our several impressions and ideas are suppos'd to have a reference. If any impression gives rise to the idea of self, that impression must continue invariably the same, thro' the whole course of our lives; since self is suppos'd to exist after that manner. But there is no impression constant and invariable. Pain and pleasure, grief and joy, passions and sensations succeed each other, and never all exist at the same time. It cannot, therefore, be from any of these impressions, or from any other, that the idea of self us deriv'd; and consequently there is no such idea.

But farther, what must become of all our particular perceptions upon this hypothesis? All these are different, and distinguishable, and separable from each other, and may be separately consider'd, and may exist separately, and have no need of any thing to support their existence. After what manner, therefore, do they belong to self; and how are they connected with it? For my part, when I enter most intimately into what I call *myself*, I always stumble on some particular perception or other, of heat or cold, light or shade, love or hatred, pain or pleasure. I can never catch *myself* at any time without a perception, and never can observe anything but the perception. When my perceptions are remov'd for any time, as by sound sleep; so long am I insensible of *myself*, and may be truly said not to exist. And were all my perceptions removed by death, and cou'd I neither think, nor feel, nor see, nor love, nor hate after the dissolution of my body, I shou'd be entirely annihilated, nor do I conceive what is farther requisite to make me a perfect non-entity.

Of the Immortality of the Soul

By the mere light of reason it seems difficult to prove the immortality of the soul. The arguments for it are commonly derived either from *metaphysical* topics, or *moral*, or *physical*. But in reality, it is the gospel, and the gospel alone, that has brought life and immortality to light.

I. Metaphysical topics are founded on the supposition that the soul is immaterial, and that it is impossible for thought to belong to a material substance.

But just metaphysics teach us that the notion of substance is wholly confused and imperfect, and that we have no other idea of any substance than as an aggregate of particular qualities, inhering in an unknown something. Matter, therefore, and spirit are at bottom equally unknown; and we cannot determine what qualities may inhere in the one or in the other.

They likewise teach us that nothing can be decided a priori concerning any cause or effect, and that experience being the only source of our judgments of this nature, we cannot know from any other principle whether matter, by its structure or arrangement, may not be the cause of thought. Abstract reasonings cannot decide any question of fact or existence.

But admitting a spiritual substance to be dispersed throughout the universe, like the ethereal fire of the *Stoics*, and to be the only inherent subject of thought, we have reason to conclude from *analogy* that nature uses it after the same manner she does the other substance, matter. She employs it as a kind of paste or clay; modifies it into a variety of forms and existences; dissolves after a time each modification; and from its substance erects a new form. As the same material substance may successively compose the body of all animals, the same spiritual substance may compose their minds: Their consciousness, or that system of thought, which they formed during life, may be continually dissolved by death; and nothing interests them in the new modification. The most positive asserters of the mortality of the soul never denied the immortality of its substance. And that an immaterial substance, as well as a material, may lose its memory or consciousness appears, in part, from experience, if the soul be immaterial.

Reasoning from the common course of nature, and without supposing any *new* interposition of the supreme cause, which is always to be excluded from philosophy; that which is incorruptible must also be ingenerable. The soul, therefore, if immortal, existed before our birth: And if the former state of existence in no wise concerned us, neither will the latter.

Animals undoubtedly feel, think, love, hate, will, and even reason tho' in a more imperfect manner than man. Are their souls also immaterial and immortal?

II. Let us now consider the *moral* arguments, chiefly those arguments derived from the justice of God, which is supposed to be further interested in the further punishment of the vicious, and reward of the virtuous.

But these arguments are grounded on the supposition that God has attributes beyond what he has exerted in this universe, with which alone we are acquainted. Whence do we infer the existence of these attributes?

It is very safe for us to affirm that whatever we know the deity to have actually done is best, but is very dangerous to affirm that he must always do what to us seems best. In how many instances would this reasoning fail us with regard to the present world?

But if any purpose of nature be clear, we may affirm that the whole scope and intention of man's creation, so far as we may judge by natural reason, is limited to his present life. With how weak a concern, from the original, inherent structure of the mind and passions, does he ever look farther? What comparison either for steadiness or efficacy, between so floating an idea, and the most doubtful persuasion of any matter of fact that occurs in common life?

There arise, indeed, in some minds, some unaccountable terrors with regard to futurity: But these would quickly vanish, were they not artificially fostered by precept and education. And those who foster them: what is their motive? Only to gain a livelihood, and to acquire power and riches in this world. Their very zeal and industry, therefore, are an argument against them.

What cruelty, what iniquity, what injustice in nature, to confine thus all our concern, as well as all our knowledge, to the present life, if there be another scene still awaiting us, of infinitely greater consequence. Ought this barbarous deceit to be ascribed to a beneficent and wise being?

Observe with what exact proportion the task to be performed and the performing powers are adjusted throughout all nature. If the reason of man gives him a great superiority above other animals, his necessities are proportionately multiplied upon him. His whole time, his whole capacity, activity, courage, passion, find sufficient employment in fencing against the miseries of his present condition. And frequently, nay almost always, are too slender for the business assigned them.

A pair of shoes, perhaps, was never yet wrought to the highest degree of perfection which the commodity is capable of attaining. Yet it is necessary, at least very useful, that there should be some politicians and moralists, even some geometers, historians, poets, and philosophers among mankind.

The powers of men are no more superior to their wants, considered merely in this life, than those of foxes and hares are, compared to *their* wants and *their* period of existence. The inference from parity of reason is therefore obvious. . ..

As every effect implies a cause, and that another, till we reach the first cause of all, which is the *Deity*, everything that happens is ordained by him, and nothing can be the object of his punishment or vengeance.

By what rules are punishments and rewards distributed? What is the divine standard of merit and demerit? Shall we suppose that human sentiments have place in the deity? However bold that hypothesis, we have no conception of any other sentiments.

According to human sentiments, sense, courage, good manners, industry, prudence, genius, &c. are essential parts of personal merit. Shall we therefore erect an Elysium for poets and heroes, like that of the ancient mythology? Why confine all rewards to one species of virtue?

Punishment, without any proper end or purpose, is inconsistent with *our* ideas of goodness and justice; and no end can be served by it after the whole scene is closed.

Punishment, according to *our* conceptions, should bear some proportion to the offense. Why then eternal punishment for the temporary offences of so frail a creature as man? Can any one approve of *Alexander's* rage, who proposed to exterminate a whole nation, because they had seized his favorite horse, *Bucephalus*?

Heaven and hell suppose two distinct species of men, the good and the bad. But the greatest part of mankind float between vice and virtue.

Were one to go round the world with an intention of giving a good supper to the righteous and a sound drubbing to the wicked, he would frequently be embarrassed in his choice and would find that the merits and demerits of most men and women scarcely amount to the value of either.

To suppose measures of approbation and blame different from the human confounds everything. Whence do we learn, that there is such a thing as moral distinctions but from our own sentiments?

What man, who has not met with personal provocation (or what good natured man who has) could inflict on crimes, from the sense of blame alone, even the common, legal, frivolous punishments? And does anything steel the breast of judges and juries against the sentiments of humanity but reflections on necessity and public interest?

By the Roman law, those who had been guilty of parricide and confessed their crime were put into a sack with an ape, a dog, and a serpent, and thrown into the river: Death alone was the punishment of those, who denied their guilt, however fully proved. A criminal was tried before *Augustus*, and condemned after full conviction: But the humane emperor, when he put the last interrogatory, gave it such a turn as to lead the wretch into a denial of his guilt. *You surely*, said the prince, *did not kill your father?* This lenity suits our natural ideas of RIGHT, even toward the greatest of criminals, and even tho' it prevents so inconsiderable a sufferance. Nay, even the most bigoted priest would naturally, without reflection, approve of it, provided the crime was not heresy or infidelity. For as these crimes hurt himself in his *temporal* interests and advantages, perhaps he may not be altogether so indulgent to them.

The chief source of moral ideas is the reflections on the interests of human society. Ought these interests, so short, so frivolous, to be guarded by punishments, eternal and infinite? The damnation of one man is an infinitely greater evil in the inverse than the subversion of a thousand million of kingdoms.

Nature has rendered human infancy peculiarly frail and mortal; as it were on purpose to refute the notion of a probationary state. The half of mankind die before they are rational creatures.

III. The *physical* arguments from the analogy of nature are strong for the mortality of the soul; and these are really the only philosophical arguments which ought to be admitted with regard to this question, or indeed any question of fact.

Where any two objects are so closely connected that all alterations which we have ever seen in the one are attended with considerable alterations in the other, we ought to conclude, by all rules of analogy, that, when there are still greater alterations produced in the former, and it is totally dissolved, there follows a total dissolution of the latter.

Sleep, a very small effect on the body, is attended with a temporary extinction; at least, a great confusion of the soul.

The weakness of the body and that of the mind in infancy are exactly so proportioned; their vigor in manhood; their sympathetic disorder in sickness; their common gradual decay in old age. The step further seems unavoidable; their common dissolution in death.

The last symptoms which the mind discovers are disorder, weakness, insensibility, stupidity, the forerunners of its annihilation. The further progress of the same causes, increasing the same effects, totally extinguish it.

Judging by the usual analogy of nature, no form can continue, when transferred to a condition of life very different from the original one, in which it was placed. Trees perish in the water; fishes in the air; animals in the earth. Even so small a difference as that of climate is often fatal. What reason then to imagine that an immense alteration, such as is made on the soul by the dissolution of its body and all its organs of thought and sensation, can be effected, without the dissolution of the whole?

Everything is in common between soul and body. The organs of the one are all of them the organs of the other. The existence therefore of the one must be dependent on that of the other.

The souls of animals are allowed to be mortal; and these bear so near a resemblance to the souls of men, that the analogy from one to the other forms a very strong argument. Their bodies are not more resembling; yet no one rejects the arguments drawn from comparative anatomy. The *Metempsychosis* is therefore the only system of this kind, that philosophy can so much as hearken to.

Nothing in this world is perpetual. Every being, however seemingly firm, is in continual flux and change: The world itself gives symptoms of frailty and dissolution: How contrary to analogy, therefore, to imagine that one single form, seemingly the frailest of any, and from the slightest of causes, subject to the greatest disorders, is immortal and indissoluble? What a daring theory is that! How lightly, not to say, how rashly entertained!

How to dispose of the infinite number of posthumous existences ought also to embarrass the religious theory. Every planet, in every solar system, we are at liberty to imagine peopled with intelligent, mortal beings: At least, we can fix on no other supposition. For these, then, a new universe must, every generation, be created, beyond the bounds of the present universe; or one must have been created at first so prodigiously wide as to admit of this continual influx of beings. Ought such bold suppositions to be received by any philosophy; and that merely on the pretence of a bare possibility?

Where it is asked whether *Agamemnon, Thersites, Hannibal, Nero,* and every stupid clown that ever existed in *Italy, Scythia, Bactria,* or *Guinea*, are now alive, can any man think, that a scrutiny of nature will furnish arguments strong enough to answer so strange a question in the affirmative? The want of arguments, without revelation, sufficiently establishes the negative.

"How much easier," says *Pliny*, "and safer for each to trust in himself, and for us to derive our idea of (future) tranquility from our experience of it before birth!" Our insensibility, before the composition of the body, seems to natural reason a proof of a like state after its dissolution.

Were our horror of annihilation an original passion, not the effect of our natural love of happiness, it would rather prove the mortality of the soul. For as nature does nothing in vain, she would never give us a horror against an impossible event. She may give us a horror against an unavoidable event, provided our endeavours, as in the present case, may often remove it to some distance. Death is in the end unavoidable, yet the human species could not be preserved, had not nature inspired us with an aversion towards it.

All doctrines are to be suspected which are favoured by our passions. And the hopes and fears which give rise to this doctrine are very obvious.

It is an infinite advantage in every controversy, to defend the negative. If the question be out of the common experienced course of nature, this circumstance is almost, if not altogether, decisive. By what arguments or analogies can we prove any state of existence which no one ever saw, and which no wise resembles any that was ever seen? Who will repose such trust in any pretended philosophy as to admit upon its testimony the reality of so marvellous a scene? Some new species of logic is requisite for that purpose, and some new faculties of the mind, which may enable us to comprehend that logic.

Nothing could set in a fuller light the infinite obligations, which mankind have to divine revelation, since we find that no other medium could ascertain this great and important truth.

HUME AND JOHNSON

Two of the giants of eighteenth-century English literature, Samuel Johnson and David Hume (who never met), held radically divergent views on many subjects, but especially about the afterlife. What follows are some remarks by Hume about his approaching death, and some testy responses by Johnson, as reported by James Boswell (1740–1795), Johnson's biographer and friend, to Hume's untroubled acceptance of death, so different from Johnson's notorious fear of it.

In spring 1775, I was struck with a disorder in my bowels, which at first gave me no alarm, but has since, as I apprehend it, become mortal and incurable. I now reckon upon a speedy dissolution. I have suffered very little pain from my disorder and, what is more strange, have, notwithstanding the great decline of my person, never suffered a moment's abatement of my spirits, insomuch that were I to name the period of my life which I should most choose to pass over again, I might be tempted to point to this later period. I possess the same ardor as ever in study, and the same gaiety in company. I consider, besides, that a man of sixty-five, by dying, cuts off only a few years of infirmities; and though I see many symptoms of my literary reputation's breaking out at least with additional luster, I knew that I could have but few years to enjoy it. It is difficult to be more detached from life than I am at present.

To conclude historically, with my own character, I am, or rather I was (for that is the style I must now use in speaking of myself, which emboldens me the more to speak my sentiments)—I was, I say, a man of mild dispositions, of command of temper, of an open, social, and cheerful humor, capable of attachment, but little susceptible of enmity, and of great moderation in all my passions. Even my love of literary fame, my ruling passion, never soured my temper, notwithstanding my frequent disappointments. My company was not unacceptable to the young and careless, as well as to the studious and literary; and, as I took a particular pleasure in the company of modest women, I had no reason to be displeased with the reception I met with from them. In a word, although most men anywise eminent have found reason to complain of calumny, I never was touched or even attacked by her baleful tooth; and though I wantonly exposed myself to the rage of both civil and religious factions, they seemed to be disarmed in my behalf of their wonted fury. My friends never had occasion to vindicate any one circumstance of my character and conduct, not but that the jealous, we may well suppose, would have been glad to invent and propagate any story to my disadvantage, but they could never find any which they thought would wear the face of probability. I cannot say there is no vanity in making this funeral oration of myself, but I hope it is not a misplaced one; and this is a matter of fact which is easily cleared and ascertained.

(April 18, 1776)

FROM BOSWELL'S *LIFE OF DR. JOHNSON*

OCTOBER 26, 1769

When we were alone, I introduced the subject of death, and endeavoured to maintain that the fear of it might be got over. I told him, that David Hume said to me, he was no more uneasy to think he should *not be* after this life, than that he *had not been* before he began to exist. JOHNSON. "Sir, if he really thinks so, his perceptions are disturbed; he is mad: if he does not think so, he lies. He may tell you, he holds his finger in the flame of a candle, without feeling pain; would you believe him? When he dies, he at least gives up all he has." BOSWELL. "Foote [Samuel Foote, 1720–1777, English actor and playwright], Sir, told me, that when he was very ill, he was not afraid to die." JOHNSON. "It is not true, Sir. Hold a pistol to Foote's breast, or to Hume's breast, and threaten to kill them, and you'll see how they behave." BOSWELL. "But may we not fortify our mind for the approach of death?" Here I am sensible I was in the wrong, to bring before his view what he ever looked upon with horror; for although when in a celestial frame, in his "Vanity of Human Wishes," [a celebrated poem by Johnson] he has supposed death to be "kind Nature's signal for retreat," from this state of being to "a happier seat," his thoughts upon this aweful change were in general full of dismal apprehensions. His mind resembled the vast amphitheatre, the Colisaeum at Rome. In the centre stood his judgement, which, like a mighty gladiator, combated those apprehensions, that, like the wild beasts of the *Arena*, were all around in cells, ready to be let out upon him. After a conflict, he drove them back into their dens; but not killing them, they were still assailing him. To my question, whether we might not fortify our minds for the approach of death, he answered, in a passion, "No, Sir, let it alone. It matters not how a man dies, but how he lives. The act of dying is not of importance, it lasts so short a time." He added, (with an earnest look,) "A man knows it must be so, and submits. It will do him no good to whine."

I attempted to continue the conversation. He was so provoked, that he said, "Give us no more of this," and was thrown into such a state of agitation, that he expressed himself in a way that alarmed and distressed me; shewed an impatience that I should leave him and when I was going away, called to me sternly, "Don't let us meet tomorrow."

TUESDAY, 16 SEPTEMBER, 1777

I mentioned to Dr. Johnson, that David Hume's persisting in his infidelity when he was dying, shocked me much. JOHNSON. "Why should it shock you, Sir? Hume owned that he had never read the New Testament with attention. Here then was a man, who had been at no pains to inquire into the truth of religion, and had continually turned his mind the other way. It was not to be expected that the prospect of death would alter his way of thinking, unless God should send an angel to set him right." I said, I had reason to believe that the thought of annihilation gave Hume no pain. JOHNSON. "It was not so, Sir. He had a vanity in being thought easy. It is more probable that he should assume an appearance of ease, than that so very improbable a thing should be as a man not afraid of going (as, in spite of his delusive theory, he cannot be sure but he may go,) into an unknown state, and not being uneasy at leaving all he knew. And you are to consider, that upon his own principle of annihilation he had no motive to speak the truth." The horrour of death which I had always observed in Dr. Johnson, appeared strong to-night. I ventured to tell him, that I had been, for moments in my life, not afraid of death; therefore I could suppose another man in that state of mind for a considerable space of time. He said, "He never had a moment in which death was not terrible to him." He added, that it had been observed, that scarce any man dies in publick, but with apparent resolution; from that desire of praise which never quits us. I said, Dr. Dodd [William Dodd, 1729–1777, a famous English preacher, executed for forgery] seemed to be willing to die, and full of hopes of happiness. "Sir, (said he,) Dr. Dodd would have given both his hands and both his legs to have lived. The better a man is, the more afraid he is of death, having a clearer view of infinite purity." He owned, that our being in an unhappy uncertainty as to our salvation, was mysterious; and said, "Ah! we must wait till we are in another state of being, to have many things explained to us." Even the powerful mind of Johnson seemed foiled by futurity. But I thought, that the gloom of uncertainty in solemn religious speculation, being mingled with hope, was yet more consolatory than the emptiness of infidelity. A man can live in thick air, but perishes in an exhausted receiver.

Dr. Johnson was much pleased with a remark which I told him was made to me by General [Pasquale] Paoli [1725–1807, Corsican patriot]:—"That it is impossible not to be afraid of death; and that those who at the time of dying are not afraid, are not thinking of death, but of applause, or something else, which keeps death out of their sight: so that all men are equally afraid of death when they see it; only some have a power of turning their sight away from it better than others."

EDWARD GIBBON (1737–1794)

O ne of the greatest English *philosophes*, Gibbon is famous for the consistent, often ironically veiled animus toward Christianity that he displayed in his monumental *History of the Decline and Fall of the Roman Empire* (1776–1778). In the following excerpt he discusses the doctrine of the immortality of the soul in classical antiquity and in the early church. Without flatly dismissing it, he makes a strong case for mortalism by heaping polite contempt on the heads of believers—pagan, Jewish, and Christian—in the afterlife.

DECLINE AND FALL OF THE ROMAN EMPIRE, VOL. I, CHAP. 15

The writings of Cicero represent in the most lively colours the ignorance, the errors, and the uncertainty of the ancient philosophers with regard to the immortality of the soul. When they are desirous of arming their disciples against the fear of death, they inculcate, as an obvious, though melancholy position, that the fatal stroke of our dissolution releases us from the calamities of life; and that those can no longer suffer who no longer exist. Yet there were a few sages of Greece and Rome who had conceived a more exalted and, in some respects, a juster idea of human nature; though it must be confessed, that, in the sublime inquiry, their reason had often been guided by their imagination, and that their imagination had been prompted by their vanity. When they viewed with complacency the extent of their own mental powers, when they exercised the various faculties of memory, of fancy, and of judgment, in the most profound speculations, or the most important labours, and when they reflected on the desire of fame, which transported them into future ages, far beyond the bounds of death and of the grave; they were unwilling to confound themselves with the beasts of the field, or to suppose, that a being, for whose dignity they entertained the most sincere admiration, could be limited to a spot of earth, and to a few years of duration. With this favorable prepossession they summoned to their aid the science, or rather the language, of Metaphysics. They soon discovered, that as none of the properties of matter will apply to the operations of the minds, the human soul must consequently be a substance distinct from the body, pure, simple and spiritual, incapable of dissolution, and susceptible of a much higher degree of virtue and happiness after the release from its corporeal prison. From these specious and noble principles, the philosophers who trod in the footsteps of Plato, deduced a very unjustifiable conclusion, since they asserted, not only the future immortality, but the past eternity of the human soul, which they were too apt to consider as a portion of the infinite and self-existing spirit, which pervades and sustains the universe. A doctrine thus removed beyond the senses and the experience of mankind might serve to amuse the leisure of a philosophic mind; or, in the silence of solitude, it might sometimes impart a ray of comfort to desponding virtue; but the faint impression which had been received in the schools, was soon obliterated by the commerce and business of active life. We are sufficiently acquainted with the eminent persons who flourished in the age of Cicero, and of the first Caesars, with their actions, their characters, and their motives, to be assured that their conduct in this life was never regulated by any serious conviction of the rewards or punishments of a future state. At the bar and in the senate of Rome the ablest orators were not apprehensive of giving offence to their hearers, by exposing the doctrine as an idle and extravagant opinion, which was rejected with contempt by every man of a liberal education and understanding.

Since therefore the most sublime efforts of philosophers can extend no farther than feebly to point out the desire, the hope, or, at most, the probability, of a future state, there is nothing except a divine revelation, that can ascertain the existence, and describe the condition of the invisible country which is destined to receive the souls of men after their separation from the body. But we must perceive several defects inherent to the popular religions of Greece and Rome, which rendered them very unequal to so arduous a task. 1. The general system of their mythology was unsupported by any solid proofs; and the wisest among the Pagans had already disclaimed its usurped authority. 2. The description of the infernal regions had been abandoned to the fancy of painters and of poets, who people them with so many phantoms and monsters, who dispensed their rewards and punishments with so little equity, that a solemn truth, the most congenial to the human heart, was oppressed and disgraced by the absurd mixture of the wildest fictions. 3. The doctrine of a future state was scarcely considered among the devout polytheists of Greece and Rome as a fundamental article of faith. The providence of the gods, as it related to public communities rather than to private individuals, was principally displayed on the visible theatre of the present world. The petitions which were offered on the altars of Jupiter or Apollo, expressed the anxiety of their worshippers for temporal happiness, and their ignorance or indifference concerning a future life. The important truth of the immortality of the soul was inculcated with more diligence as well as success in India, in Assyria, in Egypt, and in Gaul; and as we cannot attribute such a difference to the superior knowledge of the barbarians, we must ascribe it to the influence of an established priesthood, which employed the motives of virtue as the instrument of ambition.

We might naturally expect, that a principle so essential to religion, would have been revealed in the clearest terms to the chosen people of Palestine, and that it might safely have been intrusted to the hereditary priesthood of Aaron. It is incumbent on us to adore the mysterious dispensations of Providence, when we discover, that the doctrine of the immortality of the soul is darkly insinuated by the prophets, and during the long period which elapsed between the Egyptian and the Babylonian servitudes, the hopes as well as the fears of the Jews appear to have been confined within the narrow compass of the present life. After Cyrus had permitted the exiled nation to return into the promised land, and after Ezra had restored the ancient records of their religion, two celebrated sects, the Sadducees and the Pharisees, insensibly arose at Jerusalem. The former selected from the opulent and distinguished ranks of society, were strictly attached to the literal sense of the Mosaic law, and they piously rejected the immortality of the soul, as an opinion that received no countenance from the divine book, which they revered as the only rule of their faith. To the authority of scripture the Pharisees added that of tradition, and they accepted, under the name of traditions, several speculative tenets from the philosophy or religion of the eastern nations. The doctrines of fate or predestination, of angels and spirits, and of a future state of rewards and punishments, were in the number of these new articles of belief; and as the Pharisees, by the austerity of their manners, had drawn into their party the body of the Jewish people, the immortality of the soul became the prevailing sentiment of the synagogue, under the reign of the Asmonean princes and pontiffs. The temper of the Jews was incapable of contenting itself with such a cold and languid assent as might satisfy the mind of a Polytheist; and as soon as they admitted the idea of a future state, they embraced it with the zeal which has always formed the characteristic of the nation. Their zeal, however, added nothing to its evidence, or even probability; and it was still necessary, that the doctrine of life and immortality, which had been dictated by nature, approved by reason, and received by superstition, should obtain the sanction of divine truth from the authority and example of Christ.

When the promise of eternal happiness was proposed to mankind, on condition of adopting the faith, and of observing the precepts of the gospel, it is no wonder that so advantageous an offer should have been accepted by great numbers of every religion, of every rank, and of every province in the Roman empire. The ancient Christians were animated by a contempt for their present existence, and by a just confidence of immortality, of which the doubtful and imperfect faith of modern ages cannot give us any adequate notion. In the primitive church, the influence of truth was very powerfully strengthened by an opinion, which, however it may deserve respect for its usefulness and antiquity, has not been found agreeable to experience. It was universally believed, that the end of the world, and the kingdom of Heaven, were at hand. The near approach of this wonderful event had been predicted by the apostles; the tradition of it was preserved by their earliest disciples; and those who understood in their literal sense the disclosure of Christ himself, were obliged to expect the second and glorious coming of the Son of Man in the clouds, before that generation was totally extinguished, which had beheld his humble condition upon earth, and which might still be witness of the calamities of the Jews under Vespasian or Hadrian. The revolution of seventeen centuries has instructed us not to press too closely the mysterious language of prophecy and revelation; but as long as, for wise purposes, this error was permitted to subsist in the church, it was productive of the most salutary effects on the faith and practice of Christians, who lived in the awful expectation of the moment when the globe itself, and all the various races of mankind, should tremble at the appearance of the divine judge.

THE MARQUIS DE SADE (COUNT DONATIEN ALPHONSE FRANÇOIS DE SADE, 1740–1814)

F amous as a pornographer and sexual pervert, the Marquis de Sade was also a vehement atheist and mortalist; and some of his diatribes against the religious view of the afterlife are not without a certain power.

DIALOGUE BETWEEN A PRIEST AND A DYING MAN (1782)

PRIEST. Having reached this fatal moment when the veil of illusion is stripped away only to show to a man who has been misled the cruel picture of his errors and vices, my child, do you not repent at all of the disorders into which you have been swept by weakness and human frailty?

DYING MAN. Yes, my friend, I do repent.

PRIEST. Well then, profit from this blessed remorse to obtain from heaven, in the brief interval that is left to you, general absolution for your sins, and reflect that only through the mediation of the most holy sacrament of penance will it be granted to you by the Eternal One.

DYING MAN. I don't understand you, any more than you've understood me.

PRIEST – What's that?

DYING MAN. I told you that I repented.

PRIEST. I heard you.

DYING MAN. Yes, but without understanding.

PRIEST. What interpretation do you mean?

DYING MAN. Here it is. . . . Since I was created by nature with very lively tastes and very strong passions, placed in this world solely in order to surrender to them and satisfy them, and since these effects of my creation are only necessities directly related to nature's basic designs or, if you prefer, since they are all essentially derived from her plans for me, all of them by reason of her law, I repent only this: that I didn't sufficiently recognize her omnipotence; and my only remorse arises from the mediocre use that I made of the faculties (criminal according to you, quite simple according to me) that she had given me to serve her. I occasionally resisted her, and I repent that. Blinded by the absurdity of your doctrines, I took them as weapons to combat the great violence of the desire sent me by a much diviner inspiration, and I repent that: I reaped only flowers when I could have had an ample harvest of fruits. There are the just reasons for my regrets. Give me the credit of not thinking I had any others.

* * *

PRIEST. But come now, you must believe that there is something after this life? Surely your mind must have occasionally taken pleasure in piercing the thick darkness of the destiny awaiting us? And what other system could have better satisfied it than that of a multitude of punishments for those who have lived badly and an eternity of rewards for those who lived well.

DYING MAN. What system, my friend? I believe in nothingness. It has never terrified me, and I see nothing in it but consolation and simplicity. All the others are the work of pride, that one alone is the work of reason for me. Besides, nothingness is neither dreadful nor absolute. Don't I have right before my eyes the example of nature's perpetual generations and regenerations? Nothing perishes, my friend, nothing is destroyed in the world: man today, worm tomorrow, the day after tomorrow a fly; isn't that a way to go on existing? Ha! Why do you want me to be rewarded for virtues I never earned or punished for crimes I couldn't help? Can you make the goodness of your supposed God jibe with that system? And can he have wanted to create me for the pleasure of punishing me, and only as the result of a choice that he gave me no control over?

PRIEST. You are free to choose.

DYING MAN. Yes, according to your prejudices, but reason destroys them. And the system of human freedom was simply invented to underpin the system of grace, which was so flattering to your daydreams. . . . We're drawn by an irresistible force, and not for an instant do we have the power to resolve on any course except the one toward which we're already inclined. . . .

PRIEST. So the worst of all crimes shouldn't inspire us with any dread.

DYING MAN. . . . God forbid that I should seem to be encouraging crime. Surely crime must be avoided as far as possible, but it's through reason that one must learn to flee it, and not through false fears that lead nowhere, and whose effect is immediately destroyed in a soul that stands firm. Reason, my friend— yes, reason alone should warn us that harming our fellows can never make us happy; and our heart tells us that contributing to their felicity is the greatest felicity that nature has granted us on earth. . . . There you are, my friend, those are the only principles we should follow; and there's no need of a god to enjoy and admit them; all you need is a good heart. But, preacher, I feel myself growing weak, give up your prejudices, be a man, be human, without fear and without hope drop your gods and your religions too; all that is good for nothing but to put swords into the hands of men; and the mere name of all those horrors has caused more bloodshed on earth than the all other wars and all the other plagues combined. Renounce the idea of another world; there is none, none at all; but don't renounce the pleasure of being happy and of making others happy in this one. That's the only way that nature offers you of doubling and extending your existince.—My friend, voluptuousness was always the dearest thing I ever had. I have paid homage to it all my life and I've always wanted to end my life in its arms. My end draws near, six dazzlingly beautiful women are waiting in the next room, I've kept them in reserve for this moment; join in with me, try to follow my example and forget on their bosoms all the vain sophisms of superstition and all the stupid errors of hypocrisy. [The dying and the priest then join in an orgy.]

(trans. Peter Heinegg)

JOHANN WOLFGANG von GOETHE (1749–1832)

Germany's greatest poet was not a mortalist in the strict sense, and in wistful moods he liked to think that nature owed him immortality; but he also had some harsh things to say about conventional immortalists.

FROM ECKERMANN'S *CONVERSATIONS WITH GOETHE*

Apropos of *Urania* [a didactic poem on immortality by Christoph August Tiedge (1752–1841)], on February 25, 1824, Goethe remarked: "I have had a lot to endure from Tiedge's *Urania*: there was a time when people would sing and recite nothing but *Urania*. Wherever you went, you found *Urania* on everyone's table, *Urania* and immortality was the topic of every conversation. I would by no means wish to dispense with the happiness of believing in a future continuation. Indeed I would agree with Lorenzo de' Medici that all those who have no hope of another life are dead for this life as well. But such incomprehensible things lie too far away to be the object of daily meditation and thought-destroying speculation. Beyond that, if anyone believes in a continued existence, let him be happy in quiet; but he has no reason to be vain about it. Speaking of Tiedge's *Urania* I observed that, like the nobles, pious folk too form a sort of aristocracy. I found stupid women who were proud of the fact that they, like Tiedge, believed in immortality, and I had to endure some of them examining me on this point in a highly conceited manner. But I irritated them when I said it would be perfectly fine with me that after this life had run its course we were fortunate enough to have another one. I simply wanted to insist that in the beyond I wouldn't have to meet anybody who believed in it. Because then my troubles would really be starting. The pious souls would flock round me and say: 'We were right, weren't we? Didn't we predict it, didn't it all come true?'

"This being busied with thoughts of immortality is for the noble classes and especially for women with nothing to do. A solid person, though, someone who already intends to be something worthy here, and who therefore has to strive daily, has to struggle and work, gives the world to come a rest. . . . Besides, thoughts of immortality are for those who haven't done very well with happiness here; and I'd bet that if good Tiedge was enjoying a better fate, he would also have better thoughts."

Note: Alas, Goethe's own death, as we read in Richard Friedenthal, *Goethe— Sein Leben und seine Zeit* (Munich: Piper, 1963), pp. 733–734, was not so philosophically calm. Goethe's physician reports that two days before the great man died, "A piteous sight awaited me. Dreadful fear and unrest drove the very aged man (who had long been used to moving only in the most measured demeanor) with urgent haste now into the bed, where he tried in vain to find relief by changing his position every moment), now into the armchair that stood beside the bed. The pain, which settled more and more in the chest, pressed from the tortured Goethe now groans, now loud screams. The features of his face were distorted, the countenance ashen, the eyes deeply sunken into their livid hollows, dull, cloudy. The look expressed the most horrible fear of death. The whole ice-cold body dripped with sweat, the most frequent, rapid, and hard pulse could be felt; the abdomen was greatly distended, the thirst agonizing."

(trans. Peter Heinegg)

ARTHUR SCHOPENHAUER
(1788–1860)

S chopenhauer, perhaps the most thoroughgoing mortalist and pessimist ever, also happened to be a splendid writer. As someone who thought that human existence was a grievous mistake, he could not, in all consistency, grieve over the fact that life was short or that it ended forever. Nevertheless, in many passages from his works he presents a powerful case for the death of the soul.

What a great distance between our beginning and our end! The first lies in the madness of desire and the ecstasy of lust, the second in the destruction of all our organs and the smell of a decaying corpse. And the path between these two points, as far as health and the enjoyment of life go, runs constantly downhill: from the blissful dreaminess of childhood to the gaiety of youth to the strenuous toils of maturity, the often fragile wretchedness of old age, the torments of our last illness, and finally the agony of death. Doesn't it look quite as though existence were a mistake whose consequences had become gradually and increasingly obvious?

The most correct view of life would be as a *desengaño*, a disappointment: that, clearly enough, is where everything is headed.

Parerga and Paralipomena, II (1851)

We are like lambs frolicking in a meadow, while the butcher already has his eye on this one and that: for, in our good days, we have no idea what calamities fate has in store for us—sickness, persecution, impoverishment, mutilation, blinding, madness, death, etc.

Parerga and Paralipomena, II

Our existence has no solid ground to stand on except for the fleeting moment. Thus it has as its essential form constant *motion*, with no chance of attaining the rest we always strive for. It's like the course of a person running downhill: should he wish to stop, he would have to fall; and he stays upright only by continuing to run. It's like a rod balanced on one's fingertip, or a planet that would crash into its sun as soon as it ceased to rush unstoppably forward.—Hence restlessness is the hallmark of existence.

In this sort of world, where no sort of stability is possible even for an instant, and where all things are swept up in the hurly-burly of change, everything plunges ahead, races on, tries to keep its balance on the tightrope through a constant striding motion—bliss is absolutely unthinkable.

Parerga and Paralipomena, II

For every event of our life the "is" lasts only a moment, before turning into a "was." Every evening we are one day poorer. Watching this brief span of ours pass by, we might fly into a rage, but for the fact that in the profoundest depth of our being lies a secret awareness that we have an inexhaustible wellspring of eternity, from which to renew the time of life for evermore.

Reflections such as these may well serve to teach us that the greatest wisdom is to enjoy the present and to make it the goal of our life, because only the present is real; everything else is simply the idle play of thoughts. But one might just as well call it the greatest *folly*, because anything that by the next moment no longer exists, that vanishes so completely, like a dream, is never worth any serious effort.

Parerga and Paralipomena, II

Thus all the objects of the will add up to nothing. The way this becomes known and comprehensible to the intelligence rooted in each individual is, first of all, *time*. Time is the form by which this nullity of things appears to us as transitoriness. Thanks to time, all our joys and pleasures revert to nothing before our eyes, leaving us to wonder where they ever went.

from *The World as Will and Representation*, II (1818)

In early youth we sit before our future like children before the curtain in a theater, in cheerful, eager expectation of the play about to be shown. How fortunate that we don't know what really will come. Those who do know may see children as innocent offenders sentenced, not to death, but to life, as prisoners who have yet to hear the terms of their sentence.—Nevertheless everyone wants to reach a ripe old age, in other words a state where they will say: "It's bad today, and it will get worse with each succeeding day—until the very worst comes."

Parerga and Paralipomena, II

In autumn we can observe the little world of insects and see how one of them prepares a bed for itself to sleep through its long, numbing hibernation, while another spins itself into a cocoon, to spend the winter as a pupa and to awake one day in the spring, rejuvenated and fully formed. Meanwhile most insects, planning to rest peacefully in the arms of death, just take care to arrange the proper couch for their eggs, so as to come forth from them renewed at a later time. All this is nature's great lesson of immortality, which aims to show us that there is no radical difference between sleep and death, and that existence is no more threatened by the one than by the other. The care with which the insect prepares a cell or hole or nest, lays its eggs, along with food for the larvae that will emerge in the spring, and then quietly dies,—this is very much like the care with which a person sets out his clothes and his breakfast for the next morning and then quietly goes to bed. Basically this could never happen . . . unless the insect dying in the fall were just as identical with the insect that crawls out in the spring as the man lying down to sleep is with the man who rises up in the morning.

The World as Will and Representation, II

The more clearly one becomes aware of the frailty, nullity, and dreamlike nature of all things, the clearly one also becomes aware of the eternity of his own inner being. Only by contrast with this being do we recognize that nature of things, just as a passenger sees how quickly his ship is moving only by keeping an eye on the motionless shore, not by looking at the ship itself.

Parerga and Paralipomena, II

What we fear in death is by no means the pain; because, for one thing, pain obviously lies on this side of death; for another, we often flee from pain into death, just as we will sometimes endure the most dreadful pain only to escape death, even a swift and easy one, for a while longer. Thus we distinguish pain from death as two quite different things. What we fear about death, in fact, is the destruction of the individual, which is what death openly proclaims itself to be. And since the individual is the will-to-live itself in a particular objectification, it strains its whole being against death.—But where feeling leaves us helpless and abandoned, reason can nonetheless enter in and, for the most part, overcome those adverse impressions by lifting us up to a higher standpoint, whence we look not at the individual but the whole.

The World as Will and Representation, I

The terrors of death are largely based on the false appearance that in death the I disappears, and the world remains. But the opposite is rather the case: the world disappears, while the innermost core of the I, the bearer and producer of the subject, in whose representation alone the world had its existence, still persists. Along with the brain, the intellect, and with it the objective world, its mere representation, goes under. The fact that in other brains, now as before, a similar world lives on and on, is a matter of indifference with regard to the intellect that goes under.

The World as Will and Representation, II

What has been made by another has had a beginning to its existence. To claim, then, that after not existing at all for an infinite time, it will endure afterwards for all eternity is an outrageously bold assumption. If I emerged and was made from nothing for the very first time at my birth, then it's most likely that in death I will turn once again into nothing. Infinite duration *a parte post* (i.e., after death) and nothingness *a parte ante* (before birth) don't go together. Only what is itself original, eternal, and uncreated can be indestructible. The only ones with a right to despair over death are those who believe that, thirty or sixty years before, they were pure nothingness, from which they came forth as the work of another. Such people now face the difficult task of assuming that an existence which came to be in this way will go on forever—despite its having begun so late and only after an infinite period of time. On the other hand, there can be no fear of death for the person who recognizes himself as the original and eternal being, the source of all existence, and who knows that outside of him nothing really exists; who ends his original existence with the saying of the holy Upanishads, "I am all these creatures altogether, and apart from me there is no other being," in his mouth or at least in his heart. Aseity [absolute self-dependence—trans.] is the condition that insures both responsibility before the law and immortality. Thus it is in India that contempt for death and complete serenity, even joyfulness, in dying are properly at home.

The World as Will and Representation, II

In everyday social intercourse we may be asked by the sort of person who would like to know everything without learning anything, about survival after death. If so, the most appropriate, and, to put first things first, most accurate answer, would run: "After you die, you will be what you were before you were born." This implies how perverse it is to demand that an existence with a beginning should not have an end. But it also points to the fact that there may well be two forms of existence and therefore two types of nothingness. At the same time, however, one could also answer: "Whatever you will be after your death—even though that were nothing—will be just as natural and fitting as your individual, organic existence is now. So at worst the only thing you have to fear would be the moment of transition." Indeed, mature consideration of the matter shows that for a being such as ours complete nothingness would be preferable. Hence, rationally speaking, the thought that our existence will cease, or that a time will come when we shall no longer exist, should trouble us no more than the thought that we might never have come into existence. Since this existence is essentially a personal one, the end of personality should not be looked upon as a loss.

Parerga and Paralipomena, II

In truth the continuous emergence of new beings and the destruction of those in existence should be looked upon as an illusion, brought about by the apparatus of two polished lenses (brain functions), without which we can see nothing. They are called space and time and, in their interpenetration, causality. For everything that we perceive under these conditions is a mere appearance; but we don't recognize things the way they may be in themselves, that is, independent of our perception.

from *Paralipomena, Ethics*

So long as we are young—regardless of what people tell us—we take life to be endless, and so we deal with time accordingly. The older we get, the more we economize our time. For in our later years every day spent arouses a sensation like that felt at every step by a criminal being led to the gallows.

from *Maxims and Reflections* (1851)

(trans. Peter Heinegg)

WILLIAM CULLEN BRYANT
(1794–1878)

Although he lived to a ripe old age and was a successful writer and editor, Bryant's greatest achievement may well be the powerfully sententious poem on mortalism "Thanatopsis" (Vision of Death), the bulk of which he wrote when he was only sixteen years old—whence, perhaps, the tone of almost cocky self-assurance with which he bids the reader accept the prospect of eternal death without complaint.

THANATOPSIS

To him who in the love of Nature holds
Communion with her visible forms, she speaks
A various language: for his gayer hours
She has a voice of gladness, and smile
And eloquence of beauty, and she glides
Into his darker musings, with a mild
And gentle sympathy, that steals away
Their sharpness, ere he is aware. When thoughts
Of the last bitter hour come like blight
Over the spirit, and sad images
Of the stern agony, and shroud, and pall,
And breathless darkness, and the narrow house.
Make thee to shudder, and grow sick at heart,—
Go forth under the open sky, and list
To Nature's teachings, while from all around—
Earth and her waters, and the depths of air,—
Comes a still voice—Yet a few days, and thee
The all-beholding sun shall see no more
In all his course; nor yet in the cold ground,
Where thy pale form was laid, with many tears,
Nor in the embrace of ocean shall exist

Thy image. Earth, that nourished thee, shall claim
Thy growth, to be resolv'd to earth again;
And, lost each human trace, surrend'ring up
Thine individual being, thou shalt go
To mix forever with the elements,
To be a brother to th' insensible rock
And to the sluggish clod, which the rude swain
Turns with his share, and treads upon. The oak
Shall send his roots abroad, and pierce thy mould.
Yet not to thy eternal resting place
Shalt thou retire alone—nor couldst thou wish
Couch more magnificent. Thou shalt lie down
With patriarchs of the infant world—with kings
The powerful of the earth—the wise, the good,
Fair forms, and hoary seers of ages past,
All in one mighty sepulchre.—The hills
Rock-ribb'd and ancient as the sun,—the vales
Stretching in pensive quietness between;
The venerable woods—rivers that move
In majesty, and the complaining brooks
That make the meadows green; and pour'd round all,
Old ocean's grey and melancholy waste,—
Are but the solemn decorations all
Of the great tomb of man. The golden sun,
The planets, all the infinite host of heaven,
Are shining on the sad abodes of death,
Through the still lapse of ages. All that tread
The globe are but a handful to the tribes
That slumber in its bosom.—Take the wings
Of morning—and the Barcan* desert pierce,
Or lose thyself in the continuous woods
Where rills the Oregan,† and hears no sound,
Save his own dashings—yet the dead are there,
And millions in those solitudes, since first
The flight of years began, have laid them down
In their last sleep—the dead reign there alone.—
So shalt thou rest—and what if thou shalt fall
Unnoticed by the living—and no friend
Take note of thy departure? All that breathe
Will share thy destiny. The gay will laugh

---

*Libyan
†Columbia River

When thou art gone, the solemn brood of care
Plod on, and each one as before will chase
His favourite phantom, yet all these shall leave
Their mirth and their employments, and shall come,
And make their bed with thee. As the long train
Of ages glide away, the sons of men,
The youth in life's green spring, and he who goes
In the full strength of years, matron, and maid,
The bow'd with age, the infant in the smiles
And beauty of its innocent age cut off,—
Shall one by one be gathered to thy side,
By those, who in their turn shall follow them.
So live, that when thy summons comes to join
The innumerable caravan, that moves
To the pale realms of shade, where each shall take
His chamber in the silent halls of death,
Thou go not, like the quarry-slave at night,
Scourged to his dungeon, but sustain'd and sooth'd
By an unfaltering trust, approach thy grave,
Like one who wraps the drapery of his couch
About him, and lies down to pleasant dreams.

(1821)

HEINRICH HEINE (1797–1856)

A brilliant poet, journalist and critic, Heine suffered a catastrophic breakdown in 1848 from tabes dorsalis, after which he lingered in pain-ridden paralysis for eight years. From that period in his "mattress grave" he wrote a number of poems that deal with mortalism in the most intensely personal way.

FROM THE SUPPLEMENT TO "LAZARUS"

Drop those holy parables and
Pietist hypotheses:
Answer us these damning questions—
No evasions, if you please.

Why do just men stagger, bleeding,
Crushed beneath their cross's weight,
While the wicked ride the high horse,
Happy victors blessed by fate?
Who's to blame? Is God not mighty,
Not with power panoplied?
Or is evil His own doing?
Ah, that would be vile indeed.

Thus we ask and keep on asking
Till a handful of cold clay
Stops our mouths at last securely—
But pray tell, is that an answer?

(trans. Hal Draper)

Morphine

Great is the likeness of these two fair figures
Of youthful beauty, though the one appears
Much paler than the other, and much sterner—
I might say almost that he looks much nobler
Than does the other one, whose arms have held me
With such familiar warmth. How loving-soft
Was his smile then, how happy was his gaze!
It well might be that then the poppy wreath
Upon his head brushed over my own forehead
And, strangely fragrant, banished all the pain
From out my soul. But this sweet anodyne
Was of brief sway; I can be wholly healed
Only the day the older brother, he
Who is so pale and grave, lets fall his torch—
Sleep is good, yes—death is better—in truth,
The best were never to be born at all.

(trans. Hal Draper)

GIACOMO LEOPARDI
(1798–1837)

L eopardi's life was short and full of agony. Fanatical study of the classics in
his adolescence left him with a curvature of the spine that helped to bring
about his premature death. One of the supreme bards of mortalism (and possibly
the greatest poet in modern Italian literature), Leopardi produced a body of work
marked by haunting gloom and sadness. But in one of his "Little Moral Works,"
which deals with the Dutch anatomist Fredrik Ruysch (1638–1731) and his popular collection of mummies, he manages—after a somber opening chorus—to
sound a playful note.

DIALOGUE BETWEEN FREDRICK RUYSCH AND HIS MUMMIES, FROM LE OPERETTE MORALI

CHORUS OF THE DEAD

O death, you alone
are eternal in this world,
To you all things created
Turn; in you, O death,
Our naked nature comes to rest,
Not joyful, but secure,
Safe from the ancient pain. Deep night
Darkens the grave thought
In our confused mind.
The dessicated spirit
Feels the stamina wilt
in its hopes and desires.
Thus it is freed from trouble and fear
And consumes the slow and empty ages
Untouched by boredom.
We lived: and as the confused memory

Of a frightening ghost
And of a sweaty dream
Wanders in the soul
Of a nursing infant,
So the memory of our lives
Remains in us: but far from
Fear is our remembering.
What were we?
What was the bitter point
That had the name of life?
Life, we think today,
Is mysterious and stupendous;
The living think the same
Of death, the great unknown.
As when in life our naked nature
Fled from death, so now
Not joyful, but secure,
It flees the flame of life.
But fate denies happiness
Both to mortals and the dead.

RUYSCH. [*outside his study, looking through the cracks in the door*] What the devil! Who taught these dead men music, so they're singing at midnight like roosters? I'm really in a cold sweat, I'm almost deader than they are. I never thought that when I preserved them from corruption, that they'd come back to life on me. Well, that's how it is: with all my philosophy, I'm shaking from head to foot. A curse on the devil who tempted me to put these creatures in my house. I don't know what to do. If I leave them locked up in here, they might break the door down or slip out the keyhole, and come to get me in my bed? It won't look good if I call for help for fear of the dead. Oh well, let me muster some courage and put a little fear into *them*.

[*Entering.*] Children, what's the game you're playing? Have you forgotten that you're dead? What's all this ruckus about? Maybe you've gotten on your high horse because of the Tsar's visit (Ruysch's study was twice visited by Czar Peter the Great), and you suppose you're no longer bound by the same laws as before? I imagine you meant to make fun of me—you're not serious? If you *have* been resurrected, let me congratulate you; but I don't have the kind of money to support the living the way I do the dead; so get out of my house. If it's true what they say about vampires, and that's what you are, go find somebody else's blood to drink, because I'm not inclined to let you suck mine, though I was generous enough with the fake blood I put into your veins. In short, if you'll just stay quiet and silent, as you've been so far, we'll remain good friends, and you'll want for nothing in my house. Otherwise, watch out, I'll take the bar from the door, and I'll kill every one of you.

MUMMY. Don't get mad: I promise, we'll all stay as dead as we already are without your killing us.

RUYSCH. Then how did you ever get this crazy notion of singing?

MUMMY. A little while ago, just at midnight, the great mathematical year [= a cycle of 49,000 ordinary years] first ended, the one the ancients have written so much about; and likewise this is the first time that the dead can talk. And not just us, but in every cemetery, in every tomb, at the bottom of the sea, beneath the snow or the sand, under the open sky, and wherever they may be, all the dead, just like us, sang at midnight the little song you just heard.

RUYSCH. And how long will they go on singing or speaking?

MUMMY. They've already finished singing. They have permission to speak for another fifteen minutes. Then they'll return to silence until the same great year is completed.

RUYSCH. If that's true, I don't think you'll disturb my sleep the next time. So just talk freely to one another, I'll be happy to stand aside here and listen, out of curiosity, without disturbing you.

MUMMY. We can only talk in response to a living person. Those who don't have anything by way of an answer to the living fall silent as soon as the song is over.

RUSYCH. I'm truly sorry. I imagine it would be very entertaining to hear what you'd say to each other, if you could talk.

MUMMY. Even if we could, you wouldn't hear anything; because we wouldn't have anything to say to one other.

RUYSCH. A thousand questions come to mind that I'd like to ask you. But since time is short and leaves no room to choose, tell me in a few words what you felt in your body and mind at the point of death.

MUMMY. The exact point of death? I wasn't aware of it.

THE OTHER MUMMIES. Nor were we.

RUYSCH. How could you not be aware?

MUMMY. For example, just as you never notice the moment when you fall asleep, no matter how much attention you pay to it.

RUYSCH. But falling asleep is something natural.

MUMMY. And you don't think death is natural? Show me a man, an animal or a plant that doesn't die.

RUYSCH. I'm not surprised anymore that you go around singing and talking, if you didn't notice when you died. . . . I thought that when it came to this business of death, people like you would know a little more about it than the living. But, to return to my point, didn't you feel any pain at the moment of death?

MUMMY. What sort of pain would it be, if one who felt it didn't notice it?

RUYSCH. At any rate, everybody's convinced that the sensation of death is extremely painful.

MUMMY. As if death were a sensation, and not rather the opposite.

RUYSCH. And yet both those who side with the Epicureans on the nature of the soul and those who hold the common view [that the soul is immortal]—all or most of them agree with what I'm saying; they believe that death is by its very nature the most intense pain, unlike any other.

MUMMY. Well then, ask both sides on our behalf: if humans can't observe the point at which their vital functions remain merely interrupted, more or less, by sleep or lethargy or fainting or any other cause, how can they be aware of the moment when these same faculties cease completely—and not for a brief space of time, but forever? Besides, how can there be an intense sensation in death? And even more, how could death by its very nature be an intense sensation? When the capacity to feel has not only been weakened and lessened, but reduced to such an absolute minimum that it's failing and being wiped out, do you think a person could have a strong feeling? Could this very extinction of the power to feel be an overwhelming feeling? You do see that those who are dying of acute and painful diseases, as death approaches, sooner or later before they breathe their last, calm down and rest. This shows that their life, now reduced to such a tiny span, has no purchase for the pain, and so the pain stops before life does. You can tell that from us to anyone who thinks that on the point of death he'll die of pain.

RUYSCH. These arguments may satisfy the Epicureans, but not those who take a different position on the substance of the soul, as I have had in the past, and shall continue to have all the more from now on, ever since hearing the dead speak and sing. Because they believe that death consists in a separation of the soul from the body. And they can't understand how those two things, which had been joined and almost blended in such a way that they both make a single person, can be separated without tremendous violence and unspeakable anguish.

MUMMY. Tell me: is the spirit attached to the body by some nerve or muscle or membrane, which has to be broken when the spirit departs? Or is it a limb of the body that has to be violently torn or cut away? Don't you see that the soul leaves the body only insofar as it is prevented from remaining there and when there's no room left for it anymore—not because of any force that tears or uproots it? Tell me one more thing: when the soul entered, did it feel itself driven in tightly bound or, as you say, blended? Why, then, would it feel itself plucked off when it left or, if you will, feel the most shattering sensation? You can be sure that the entrance and the exit of the soul are equally quiet, easy, and gentle.

RUYSCH. Then what is death, if not pain?

MUMMY. Pleasure more than anything. You have to know that dying, like falling asleep, doesn't take place in a single instant, but by degrees. It's true that these degrees are more or less, greater or less, according to the various causes and kinds of death. At the last of these moments, death brings no more pain or pleasure than sleep. In the moments that precede it, it can't cause pain, because pain is something vital; and by that time, namely when dying has begun, a person's senses are dying too, that is, enormously weakened. Death may well be a cause for pleasure; because pleasure is *not* always something vital. The majority of human pleasures may, in fact, consist in a kind of languor. So a person's senses are capable of pleasure even when they are close to extinction, since languor itself is very often a pleasure, especially when it frees you from suffering. You know well that the cessation of any pain or discomfort is itself a pleasure. So the languor of death should be all the more welcome, the more suffering it frees a man from. For myself, even though in the hour of my death I didn't pay much attention to what I was feeling, because the doctors had forbidden me to tire my brain, I do remember that the sensation I had wasn't much different from the pleasure caused by the languor of sleep when one is dozing off.

THE OTHER MUMMIES. We too seem to remember as much.

RUYSCH. Have it your way: although all those with whom I've ever discussed this subject voiced a very different opinion. But, as so far as I recall, they didn't cite their own experience. Now tell me: in the hour of death, when you felt that sweetness, did you think you were dying and that the pleasure was a courtesy on death's part? Or did something else cross your mind?

MUMMY. As long I wasn't dead, I was never convinced that I wouldn't escape that danger; and up to the last moment that I had the power to think, I hoped that I had at least an hour or two left, as I believe happens to many people when they are dying.

THE OTHER MUMMIES. The same thing happened to us.

RUYSCH. That's what Cicero says: no one is too decrepit not to promise himself at least one more year of life. But how could you finally tell that the spirit had left the body? How did you know that you were dead? They don't answer. Children, don't you hear me? The fifteen minutes must be up. Let's feel their pulse a bit. They're dead again all right; there's no danger that they'll frighten me another time. Let's go back to bed.

(Composed in 1824, first published in 1827)

(trans. Peter Heinegg)

---

*See Fontanelle, Eloge de mons. Rusych. The means used by Ruysch to preserve his corpses consisted in injections of a certain fluid which he himself prepared, which had a miraculous effect. (note by Leopardi)

EDWARD FITZGERALD
(1809–1883)

That a mid-Victorian poet should openly proclaim the futility of life and the finality of death, as well as repeatedly encourage his readers to indulge in alcohol and sex (with a "beloved" of unspecified gender) might have been extremely shocking. But since the retiring, independently wealthy dilettante Edward FitzGerald was only translating the work of a Muslim heretic, the late eleventh-early twelfth century Persian astronomer and hedonist, Omar Khayyám, the scandal was minimal. First published in 1859, and later revised and expanded, the *Rubáiyát* has a unique place in English literature as the ultimate "exotic" classic of mortalism.

FROM *THE RUBÁIYÁT OF OMAR KHAYYÁM OF NAISHÁPÚR*

13

Some for the Glories of this World; and some
Sigh for the Prophet's Paradise to come;
        Ah, take the Cash, and let the Credit go,
Nor heed the rumble of a distant Drum!

15

And those who husbanded the golden Grain,
And those who flung it to the winds like Rain,
        Alike to no such aureate Earth are turned
As, buried once, Men want dug up again.

14

Look to the blowing* Rose about us—"Lo,
"Laughing," she says, "into the world I blow,
    "At once the silken Tassel of my Purse
"Tear, and its Treasure on the Garden throw."

16

The worldly hope men set their Hearts upon
Turns Ashes—or it prospers; and anon,
    Like Snow upon the Desert's dusty Face,
Lighting a little hour or two—is gone.

17

Think, in this battered Caravanserai
Whose Portals are alternate Night and Day,
    How Sultán after Sultán with his Pomp
Abode his destined Hour, and went his way.

21

Ah, my Belovéd, fill the Cup that clears
TODAY of past regrets and future Fears:
    Tomorrow!—Why, Tomorrow I may be
Myself with Yesterday's Sevn Thousand Years.

22

For some we loved, the loveliest and the best
That from his Vintage rolling Time hath prest,
    Have drunk their Cup a Round or two before,
And one by one crept silently to rest.

23

And we, that make merry in the Room
They left, and Summer dresses in new bloom,
    Ourselves must we beneath the Couch of Earth
Descend—ourselves to make a Couch—for whom?

---

*blooming

24

Ah, make the most of what we yet may spend,
Before we too into the Dust descend;
     Dust into Dust, and under Dust to lie,
Sans Wine, sans Song, sans Singer, and sans End!

25

Alike for those who for TODAY prepare,
And those that after some TOMORROW stare,
     A Muezzin from the Tower of Darkness cries,
"Fools! your Reward is neither Here nor There."

26

Why, all the Saints and Sages who discussed
Of the Two Worlds so wisely—they are thrust
     Like foolish Prophets forth; their Words to Scorn
Are scattered, and their Mouths are stopt with Dust.

35

Then to the lip of this poor earthen Urn
I leaned, the Secret of my Life to learn;
     And Lip to Lip it murmured—"While you live,
Drink!—for, once dead, you never shall return."

63

Oh threats of Hell and Hopes of Paradise!
One thing at least is certain—*This* Life flies;
     One thing is certain and the rest is Lies;
The Flower that once has blown for ever dies.

64

Strange, is it not? that of the myriads who
Before us passed the door of Darkness through,
     Not one returns to tell us of the Road,
Which to discover we must travel too.

65

The Revelations of Devout and Learned
Who rose before us, and as Prophets burned,
    Are all but Stories, which, awoke from Sleep
They told their comrades, and to Sleep returned.

66

I sent my Soul through the Invisible,
Some letter of that Afterlife to spell:
    And by and by my Soul returned to me,
And answered "I Myself am Heav'n and Hell:"

67

Heavn'n but the Vision of fulfilled Desire,
And Hell the Shadow from a Soul on fire,
    Cast on the Darkness into which Ourselves,
So late emerged from, shall so soon expire.

68

We are no other than a moving row
Of Magic Shadow-shapes that come and go
    Round with the Sun-illumined Lantern held
In Midnight by the Masters of the Show;

69

But helpless Pieces of the Game He plays
Upon his Checkerboard of Nights and Days;
    Hither and thither moves, and checks, and slays,
And one by one back in the Closet lays.

71

The moving Finger writes; and, having writ,
Moves on; nor all your Piety nor Wit
    Shall lure it back to cancel half a Line,
Nor all your Tears wash out a Word of it.

72

And that inverted Bowl they call the Sky,
Whereunder crawling cooped we live and die,
    Lift not your hands to *It* for help—for It
As impotently moves as you or I.

99

Ah, Love! Could you and I with Him* conspire
To grasp this sorry Scheme of Things entire,
    Would we not shatter it to bits—and then
Remold it nearer to the Heart's Desire.

---

* the "stern Recorder" of the "Roll of Fate" (98)

SØREN KIERKEGAARD
(1813–1855)

L ike Pascal before him and Unamuno after him (see "The Hunger for Immortality" in *The Tragic Sense of Life*), Kierkegaard was a believer whose anxieties could be more revealing than his certainties. In the following brief excerpt from the Danish philosopher-theologian's "Speech in Praise of Abraham," from *Fear and Trembling* (1843), Kirkegaard looks into the abyss before taking the leap of faith over it, leaving the reader with the impression that his affirmation is willful and desperate rather than rationally justified.

FROM *FEAR AND TREMBLING*

If there were no eternal consciousness in man, if at the bottom of everything there were only a wild element, a power that, twisting in dark passions, produced everything great or consequential; if an unfathomable, insatiable emptiness lay hid beneath everything, what would life be but despair? If it were thus, if there were no sacred bond uniting mankind, if one generation rose up after another like the leaves of the forest [see Glaucus' speech to Diomedes in section 3, on Homer—ed.], if one generation succeeded the other as the song of birds in the woods, if the human race passed through the world as a ship through the sea or the wind through the desert, a thoughtless and fruitless whim, if an eternal oblivion always lurked hungrily for its prey and there were no power strong enough to wrest it from its clutches—how empty and devoid of comfort life would be!

(trans. Alistair Hannay)

GUSTAVE FLAUBERT
(1821–1880)

In the short masterpiece of his last years, *Three Tales* Flaubert, a lifelong unbeliever, told three lives of saints, working backwards from a contemporary illiterate peasant woman, Félicité, through the legendary medieval saint, Julian the Hospitaller, to John the Baptist. Flaubert genuinely admires the soulful religious passion of his protagonists, but they are all deluded. Félicité mistakes her stuffed pet parrot for the Holy Ghost, Julian culminates his ascetical martyrdom by rapturously embracing a leper, who is Jesus in disguise, and sailing off with him into heaven—but only on a stained glass window—while the brutal execution of John the Baptist is just one more meaningless act of violence in the cacophony and moral chaos swirling around the reign of Herod Antipas in first-century Palestine.

In the first of these three absurd death scenes, Félicité is expiring from pneumonia as the Corpus Christi procession winds through the little Norman town of Pont-l'Évêque. This ritual involves carrying the consecrated communion host in a large golden monstrance, depositing it briefly on various makeshift "altars of repose," and adoring the Divine Presence. On "her" altar Félicité has placed her most precious possession, the moldy carcass of her parrot Loulou. As a devout mortalist and ex-Catholic, Flaubert finds the whole tribal scene touchingly human (far more appealing, say, than an afternoon at the Stock Exchange) and, of course, utterly grotesque.

FROM *A SIMPLE HEART* (1877)

She hardly ever went out now, so as to avoid the bric-a-brac dealer's store, where some of her old furniture was on display. Ever since her attack of vertigo, she dragged one leg; and, as her strength diminished, mère Simon, whose grocery store had gone under, came every morning to chop her wood and pump some water.

Her eyesight grew weaker. The window blinds didn't open anymore. More years passed. And the house found no one to buy or rent it.

Afraid that she might be thrown out, Félicité never asked for any repairs. The roof laths rotted; for an entire winter her bolster was soaked. After Easter she began spitting blood.

Then mère Simon called a doctor. Félicité wanted to know what she had. But, too deaf to hear, the only word to get though to her was "pneumonia." She was familiar with it, and she softly replied:—"Ah! Like Madame!" finding it natural that she would follow her mistress.

The time for the altars of repose was approaching.

The first one was always at the bottom of the hill, the second in front of the post office, and the third about halfway down the street. There were rivalries about that one; and the women of the parish finally chose Madame Aubain's courtyard.

Her fever and difficulty in breathing increased. Félicité was distressed that she couldn't do anything for the altar of repose. If only she could have put something there. Then she thought of the parrot. That wasn't proper, the neighbors objected; but the curé gave her permission. She was so happy that she asked him to accept, after her death, the gift of Loulou, her only treasure.

From Tuesday to Saturday, the vigil of Corpus Christi, her coughing worsened. In the evening her face looked shriveled, her lips stuck to her gums, she began to vomit. And the next day, feeling very low, she sent for a priest.

Three good women stood round her as the last rites were administered. Then she declared that she needed to speak to Fabu,

He arrived in his Sunday best, ill at ease in that dismal setting.

—"Forgive me," she said as she tried to reach out her arm, "I thought you were the one who killed him!"

What was gossip like that supposed to mean? Suspecting him of a murder, a man like him! And he grew indignant, and started to make a fuss.—"She's out of her mind now, you can tell!"

From time to time Félicité would say things to shadows. The good women left. Mère Simon ate her lunch.

A little later she took Loulou and brought him up to Félicité:

—"Come on now! Say goodbye to him!"

Even though he wasn't a corpse, he was all eaten up by worms; one of his wings was broken; the stuffing was coming out of his abdomen. But, blind as she was now, she kissed him on the forehead and pressed him against her cheek. Mère Simon took him away to place him on the altar of repose.

* * *

The meadows wafted the smells of summer; flies buzzed; the sun made the river glisten, and it warmed the slates. Mère Simon, now back in the room, was nodding off.

The ringing of the bells woke her up; they were leaving the church after Vespers. Félicité's delirium lifted. As she thought of the procession, she watched it as if she had been following after.

All the schoolchildren, the choirboys, and the firemen went marching along the sidewalks while in the middle of the street advanced in the front: the verger, armed with his halberd, the beadle with a large cross, the schoolmaster keeping an eye on the boys, the nun worried about her little girls; three of the prettiest, their hair curled like angels, were tossing rose petals in the air; the deacon, with outstretched arms, conducted the band; and two thurifers turned round at every step to face the Blessed Sacrament, which was carried, beneath a canopy of flame-colored velvet held by four churchwardens, by Monsieur le curé, wearing his fine chasuble. A flood of people swept along behind, between the white cloths covering the walls of the houses; and they arrived at foot of the hill.

A cold sweat soaked Félicité's temples. Mère Simon wiped it off with a cloth, telling herself that some day she too would have to pass that way.

The murmur of the crowd swelled, got very loud for moment, then faded.

A burst of gunfire shook the windows. It was the postilions saluting the monstrance. Félicité rolled her eyes, and said, in the loudest voice she could manage: "Is he all right?"—she was tormented about the parrot.

Her agony began. A death rattle, coming faster and faster, made her midriff shudder. Bubbles of froth appeared at the corners of her mouth, and her whole body trembled.

Soon the oompahpah of the ophicleides could be heard, the clear voices of the children, the deep voices of the men. They all fell silent from time to time, and the tramping of feet, muffled by flowers, sounded like a flock ambling over grass.

The clergy appeared in the courtyard. Mère Simon got on a chair to reach the little circular window and look down on the altar of repose.

Green garlands hung on the altar, which was decorated with a furbellow of needlepoint English lace. In the middle was a little frame containing relics, two orange trees at the corners, and all along the way silver candlesticks and china vases, from which sprouted sunflowers, lilies, peonies, foxgloves, and clusters of hydrangea. This heap of dazzling colors poured down from the first floor to the carpet spread over the paving stones; and some rare objects caught the eye. A silver-gilt sugar bowl had a coronet of violets, pendants of Alençon gems gleamed on a bed of moss, two Chinese screens showed off their landscapes. Loulou, hidden beneath some roses, was invisible except for his blue brow, like a plaque of lapis-lazuli.

The vestrymen, the choirboys, and the children, were ranged around the three sides of the courtyard. The priest slowly walked up the steps and placed on the lace his great golden sun, which beamed. Everyone knelt. There was a great silence. Then the censers, swinging away, slid up and down their chains.

A vapor of blue incense rose up to Félicité's room. She thrust her nostrils forward as she inhaled it with a mystical sensuality, then closed her eyes. Her lips smiled. Her heartbeats slowed, one by one, fainter each time, softer, like a fountain running dry, like an echo drifting away; and when she breathed her last, she thought she saw, in the half-opened heavens, a gigantic parrot hovering over her head.

(trans. Peter Heinegg)

LEO TOLSTOY (1828–1910)

Tolstoy's long and incredibly productive career is often seen as incarnated in two very different figures, the epic novelist and the angry moralist, divided by the gulf of the profound personal crisis he endured in the mid–1870s. As described in *A Confession* (1879), Tolstoy's growing obsession with death (and the mockery it made of all human endeavors) forced him (ostensibly) to turn his back on art and cobble together an idiosyncratic, vaguely deistic religion preaching altruism and the simple life. Although his later didactic work, such as the deservedly famous "The Death of Ivan Ilych" (1886), never matched the splendor and scope of *War and Peace* (1862–1869), it also shows many signs of the master's touch. The evidence suggests that unlike the desperately fideistic believer Dostoyevsky, Tolstoy was at heart a mortalist; in any case his visions of death's terror carry far more weight than the deus ex machina consolations that he felt obliged to offer at the end of "The Death of Ivan Ilych" and the later, parallel story, "Master and Man" (1895).

FROM CHAPTER 4 OF *A CONFESSION*

My life came to a standstill. I could breathe, eat, drink, or sleep—and I couldn't help breathing, eating, drinking, and sleeping, But there was no life because I had no desires whose gratification I would have found reasonable. If I wanted anything, I knew in advance that whether or not I satisfied my wish, nothing would come of it.

If an enchantress had come and offered to make my wishes come true, I wouldn't have known what to say. If in moments of drunkenness I had, not desires, but habits left behind by old desires; in my sober moments I knew that this was a fraud. There was nothing to wish for, I couldn't even wish to know the truth, since I had already guessed what it consisted in. The truth was that life is meaningless.

I seemed to have gone on living and walking, and then I came to the edge of an abyss and saw clearly that there was nothing in front of me but destruction. There was no stopping, and no going back, and no closing my eyes lest I see that nothing lay before me but the delusions of life and happiness, and real suffering and real death—complete annihilation.

Life became hateful to me. Some irresistible force was drawing me on to rid myself of life, one way or another. I can't say I "wished" to kill myself. The force pulling me away from life was more powerful, more sustained, and more encompassing than any wish. It was like my old yearning for life, only in reverse. I was striving with all my energy to flee from life. The thought of suicide now came as naturally to my mind as the thoughts of bettering my life had once come before. And the idea was so seductive that I had to use cunning against myself lest I put it into effect too quickly, I didn't want to hurry, only because I wanted to expend every effort to straighten myself out. "If I can't get out of this tangle," I told myself, "there'll always be time." And so it was that I, a happy man, had to take a rope out of my room, where I undressed by myself every evening, lest I hang myself from the crossbeam between the two closets. And I stopped going out to hunt with a gun, to avoid the temptation of such an easy way to get rid of my life. I myself didn't know what I wanted. I was afraid of life, I struggled to get free from it, and meanwhile I still hoped for something from it.

All this happened at a time when I was surrounded by what people consider perfect happiness: I was not yet fifty. I had a good wife who loved me, as I loved her, fine children, a large estate, which was growing and increasing without effort on my part. I was respected by friends and acquaintances. More than ever I was praised by other people, and without unduly flattering myself I could say that I had achieved fame. With all this, not only wasn't I sickly in body or mind, but on the contrary I enjoyed such physical and mental strength as I've rarely met in men my age. I could do eight to ten hours of mental work at a stretch, without suffering any ill effects from such exertion. And in this situation I had gotten to the point that I couldn't live, and since I feared death, I had to outfox myself so as not to take my life.

My mental state could have been summed up this way: my life is some sort of stupid nasty joke someone has played on me. Apart from the fact that I didn't recognize any "someone" who might have created me, this way of putting it, that in bringing me into the world someone had played a stupid, malicious trick on me, was the one I found most natural.

I couldn't help imagining that somewhere someone was amusing himself by watching me live for a full thirty or forty years—learning, developing, growing in body and mind, And now that my mind was fully mature, now that I had reached the summit of life, from which I saw everything laid out before me— how like a total fool I stood there at the summit clearly perceiving that there was nothing in life, that there never had been and never would be. "But he thinks it's funny. . . ."

But whether or not someone laughing at me really existed, it didn't make things any easier for me. I wouldn't attach any rational significance either to a single act or to my whole life. The one thing that surprised me was that I had failed to grasp this right from the start. Everybody else had known it for ages. If not today then tomorrow, disease and death would come (they had come already) to those dear to me and to myself, and nothing would be left but the stench and the worms. All my affairs, whatever they might be, would sooner or later be forgotten, and I would be gone too. So why trouble oneself about it? How can man not see this and just go on living? That was the amazing thing. You could only live as long as you were drunk with life. Once you sobered up, you couldn't fail to see that all this was a cheat, and a stupid cheat at that. That is precisely why there was nothing laughable or witty about it; it was all cruel and stupid.

There's an old Eastern tale [from the eleventh-century Greek legend of Barlaam and Ioasaph, a Christian version of the life of the Buddha—ed.] told about a traveler overtaken on the steppe by a raging beast. To save himself from the beast, the traveler leaps into a dry well, but at the bottom of the well he sees a dragon with gaping jaws which threaten to devour him. The unfortunate man, not daring to climb out lest he be devoured by the dragon, clutches on to the branch of a wild shrub growing out of the clefts in the well, and seizes hold of it. His hands grow weak, and he senses that soon he'll have to surrender to the doom that awaits him at the top and on the bottom. But he still holds on, and as he does, he looks around and sees that two mice, one black and the other white, are gnawing their way around the main stem of the bush he's hanging from. Any moment now the branch will snap and be torn away, and he'll fall into the dragon's jaws. The traveler sees this and knows he'll inevitably perish, but, while he's hanging there he searches around him and finds a few drops of honey on the leaves of the bush. He reaches them with his tongue and licks them up. And so I clung to the branch of life, knowing that the dragon of death was inevitably waiting for me, ready to tear me to pieces. And I couldn't understand why I had fallen into this torment, I tried to suck that honey, which used to console me, but it no longer gave me joy. And the white mouse and the black mouse (day and night) gnawed away at my branch. I saw the dragon clearly, and the honey was no longer sweet to my taste. I saw only the inescapable dragon and the mice, and I couldn't tear my eyes away from them. This was no fable. It was the real, incontestable truth, a truth that everyone could understand.

The old delusive joys of life, which used to assuage my terror of the dragon, no longer deceived me. You could say to me as often as you liked, "You can't understand the meaning of life—don't think, live!" I couldn't do that because I had done it for too long before. Now I couldn't fail to see day and night hurrying on and leading me to death. I saw only that, because that alone was the truth. All the rest was a lie. The two drops of honey, which had turned my glance away from the cruel truth longer than anything else (my love of family and of writing), were no longer sweet.

"Family . . . ," I said to myself. But my family—my wife and children— were also people. They found themselves in the same position I was in. They had either to live in a lie or see the terrible truth. Why should they live? Why should

I love them, care for them, raise them, watch over them? To feel the same despair I felt, or to stupefy themselves? If I loved them, I couldn't conceal the truth from them. Every step forward in knowledge brought them closer to the truth. But the truth was death.

"Art, poetry? . . ." For a long time, under the sway of success and the praise I received, I tried to convince myself that this was something I could do, even though death would come to annihilate everything, myself, my affairs, and any memory of them. But I soon came to see that this too was a delusion. It was clear to me that art was an embellishment of life, an enticement to life. But life had lost its attractiveness to for me, so how could I attract others to it? So long as the life I led wasn't my own, but an alien existence on whose waves I was borne along; so long as I believed that life had a meaning even though I couldn't spell it out, every reflection of life in poetry and art gave me pleasure, and I enjoyed looking at life in the mirror of art. But when I began to search for the meaning of life, when I felt the need to live my own life, that mirror began to strike me as either unnecessary (superfluous and ridiculous) or painful, I could no longer take heart from what I saw in the mirror—I saw that my position was stupid and desperate. It was all very well to enjoy the mirror when in the depths of my soul I believed that my life had a meaning. Then that play of lights and shadows—the comic, the tragic, the touching, the beautiful and the terrible things in life— brought me amusement. But once I knew that life was meaningless and horrible, the patterns in the mirror could divert me no longer. Honey had no sweetness for me when I saw the dragon, and the mice gnawing away at my support.

But that wasn't all. If I had simply understood that life was meaningless, I might have quietly accepted the fact, knowing that it was my destiny. But I couldn't rest content with that. Had I been like a man living in a forest, from which he knows there is no way out, I might have been able to live. But I was like a man lost in the forest: terrified to be lost, he rushes about, hoping to get to the road, he knows that each step only leads him farther astray, but he can't help rushing about.

How terrible that was. And to free myself from this terror I wished to kill myself. I felt terror in the face of what awaited me, and I knew that the terror was worse than the situation itself, but I couldn't dispel it, and I couldn't wait patiently for the end. And however convincing it might be to reflect that whether a blood vessel burst in my heart or something or other ruptured, it would in any event be all over, I couldn't wait patiently for the end. My terror of the darkness was too great, and I longed to free myself from it with a noose or a bullet as soon as possible. And this feeling, more than anything else, drew me on toward suicide.

(trans. Peter Heinegg)

FROM *THE DEATH OF IVAN ILYCH*

Ivan Ilych saw that he was dying, and he was in continual despair.

In the depth of his heart he knew he was dying, but not only was he not accustomed to the thought, he simply did not, and could not grasp it.

The syllogism he had learnt from Kiezewetter's Logic: "Caius is a man, men are mortal, therefore Caius is mortal," had always seemed to him correct as applied to Caius, but certainly not as applied to himself. That Caius——man in the abstract—was mortal, was perfectly correct, but he was not Caius, nor an abstract man, but a creature quite, quite separate from all others. He had been little Vanya, with a mama and a papa, with Mitya and Volodya, with the toys, a coachman and a nurse, afterwards with Katenka and with all the joys, griefs, and delights of childhood, boyhood, and youth. What did Caius know of the smell of that striped leather ball Vanya had been so fond of? Had Caius kissed his mother's hand like that, and did the silk of her dress rustle so for Caius? Had he rioted like that at school when the pastry was bad? Had Caius been in love like that? Could Caius preside at a session as he did? "Caius really was mortal, and it was right for him to die, but for me, little Vanya, Ivan Ilych, with all my thoughts and emotions, it's altogether a different matter. It cannot be that I ought to die. That would be too terrible."

Such was his feeling.

"If I had to die like Caius, I should have known it was so. An inner voice would have told me so, but there was nothing of the sort in me, and I and all my friends felt that our case was quite different from that of Caius. And now here it is!" he said to himself, "It can't be. It's impossible! But here it is. How is this? How is one to understand it?"

He could not understand it, and tried to drive this false, incorrect, morbid thought away and to replace it with other proper and healthy thoughts. But that thought, and not the thought only but the reality itself, seemed to come and confront him.

And to replace that thought he called up a succession of others, hoping to find in them some support. He tried to get back into the former current of thoughts that had once screened the thought of death from him. But strange to say, all that had formerly shut off, hidden, and destroyed his consciousness of death, no longer had that effect. Ivan Ilych now spent most of his time in attempting to re-establish that old current. He would say to himself: "I will take up my duties again——after all I used to live by them." And banishing all doubts he would go to the law courts, enter into conversations with his colleagues, and sit carelessly as was his wont, scanning the crowd with a thoughtful look and leaning both his emaciated arms on the arms of his oak chair; bending over as usual to a colleague and drawing his papers nearer he would interchange whispers with him, and then suddenly raising his eyes and sitting erect would pronounce certain words and open the proceedings. But suddenly in the midst of those proceedings the pain in his side, regardless of the stage the proceedings had reached, would begin its own gnawing work. Ivan Ilych would turn his attention to it and try to drive the thought of it away, but without success. *It* would come and stand before him and look at him, and he would be petrified and the light would die out of his eyes, and he would again begin asking himself whether *It* alone was true, And his colleagues and subordinates would see with surprise and distress that he, the brilliant and subtle judge, was becoming confused and making mistakes. He would shake himself, try to pull himself together, manage somehow to bring the session to a close, and return home with the sorrowful consciousness that his judicial labors could not as formerly hide from him what he wanted them to hide, and could not deliver him from *It*. And what was worst of all was that *It* drew his attention to itself not in order to make him take some action but only that he should look at *It*, look it straight in the face, look at it, and without doing anything, suffer inexpressibly.

And to save himself from this condition Ivan Ilych looked for consolations——new screens——and new screens were found and for a while seemed to save him, but then that immediately fell to pieces or rather became transparent, as if *It* penetrated them and nothing could veil *It*.

In these latter days he would go into the drawing-room he had arranged—that drawing room where he had fallen and for the sake of which (how bitterly ridiculous it seemed) he had sacrificed his life—for he knew that his illness originated with that knock. He would enter and see that something had scratched the polished table. He would look for the cause of this and find that it was the bronze ornamentation of an album that had got bent. He would take up the expensive album, which he had lovingly arranged, and feel vexed with his daughter and her friends for their untidiness—for the album was torn here and there and some of the photographs turned upside down. He would put it carefully in order and bend the ornamentation back into position. Then it would occur to him to place all those things in another corner of the room. Near the plants, he would call the footman, but his daughter or wife would come to help him. They would not agree, and his wife would contradict him, and he would dispute and grow angry. But that was all right, for then he did not think about *It*. *It* was invisible.

But then, when was moving something himself, his wife would say: "Let the servants do it. You will hurt yourself again," And suddenly *It* would flash through the screen and he would see it. It was just a flash, and he hoped it would disappear, but he would involuntarily pay attention to his side. "It sits there as before, gnawing just the same!" And he could no longer forget *It*, but could distinctly see it looking at him from behind the flowers. "What is it all for"?

"It really is so! I lost my life over that curtain as I might have done when storming a fort. Is that possible? How terrible, and how stupid. It can't be true! It can't, but it is."

He would go to his study, lie down, and again be alone with *It*: face to face with *It*. And nothing could be done with *It* except to look at it and shudder.

(trans. Aylmer Maude)

EMILY DICKINSON (1830–1886)

In poems that ironically borrow from the strophic forms of Protestant hymns, Emily Dickinson denies the Christian creed ("The Bible is an antique Volume— / Written by faded Men / At the suggestion of Holy Specters—") and its consolations.

Her confrontations with death, not as doorway to Paradise but as trapdoor to Nothingness, have a unique vividness and honesty.

216

Safe in their Alabaster Chambers—
Untouched by Morning
And untouched by Noon—
Sleep the meek members of the Resurrection—
Rafter of satin,
And Roof of stone.

Grand go the Years—in the Crescent—above them—
Worlds scoop their Arcs—
And firmaments—row
Diadems—drop—and Doges—surrender—
Soundless as dots—on a Disc of Snow—

(1861)

280

I felt a Funeral, in my Brain,
And Mourners to and fro
Kept treading—treading—till it seemed
That Sense was breaking through—
And when they all were seated,
A Service like a Drum—

Kept beating—beating—till I thought
My Mind was going numb—

And then I heard them lift a Box
And creak across my Soul
With those same boots of Lead, again,
Then Space—began to toll,

As all the Heavens were a Bell,
And Being, but an Ear,
And I, and Silence, some strange Race
Wrecked, solitary, here—

And then a Plank in Reason, broke
And I dropped down, and down—
And hit a World, at every plunge,
And finished knowing—then—

(ca. 1861)

465

I heard a Fly buzz—when I died—
The Stillness in the Room
Was like the Stillness in the Air—
Between the Heaves of Storm—

The Eyes around—had wrung them dry—
And breaths were gathering firm
For that last Onset—when the King
Be witnessed—in the Room—
I willed my Keepsakes—Signed away
What portion of me be
Assignable—and then it was
There interposed a Fly—

With blue—uncertain stumbling Buzz—
Between the light—and me—
And then the Windows failed—and then
I could not see to see—

(ca. 1862)

712

Because I could not stop for Death—
He kindly stopped for me—
The Carriage held but just Ourselves—
And Immortality,

We slowly drove—He knew no haste
And I had put away
My labor and my leisure too,
For his Civility—

We passed the School, where Children strove
At Recess—in the Ring—
We passed the Fields of Gazing Grain—
We passed the Setting Sun—

Or rather—He passed Us—
The Dews drew quivering and chill—
For only Gossamer, my Gown—
My Tippet*—only Tulle†—
We passed before a House that seemed
A Swelling of the Ground—
The Roof was scarcely visible—
The Cornice in the Ground—

Since then—'tis Centuries—and yet
Feels shorter than the Day
I first surmised the Horses' Heads
Were toward Eternity—

(ca. 1863)

---

*shoulder cape
†thin fabric

ALGERNON CHARLES SWINBURNE (1837–1909)

The drunken, debauched Swinburne, who crashed in his thirties but survived into his seventies, wrote his best poetry as a young man, when he sang his dark pagan odes to mortalism. Swinburne's heavy-breathing lushness, his willingness to sacrifice clear-cut sense to all-engulfing sound, can make him faintly laughable, but his work has very real power. He loved to invoke Proserpine, the wife of Pluto and Queen of Hades, as a symbol of sweet eternal oblivion. In "Hymn to Proserpine" he speaks in the voice of the (dying) emperor Julian the Apostate (reigned 361–363 C.E.), the last pagan emperor, who concedes that Jesus has defeated him but foresees the end of Christianity and revels in the somber truth of mortalism.

HYMN TO PROSERPINE
(After the Proclamation of the Christian Faith)
Vicisti, Galilaee

I have lived long enough, having seen one thing, that love hath
    an end;
Goddess and maiden and queen, be near me now and befriend.
Thou art more than the day or the morrow, the seasons that
    laugh or that weep;
For these give joy and sorrow; but thou, Proserpina, sleep.
Sweet is the treading of wine, and sweet the feet of the dove;
But a goodlier gift is thine than the foam of the grapes or love.
Yea, is not even Apollo, with hair and harpstring of gold,
A bitter god to follow, a beautiful god to behold?
I am sick of singing; the bays burn deep and chafe. I am fain
To rest a little from praise and grievous pleasure and pain.
For the gods we know not, who give us our daily breath,
We know they are cruel as love or life, and lovely as death.

O gods dethroned and deceased, cast forth, wiped out in a day!
From your wrath is the world released, redeemed from your chains,
    men say.
New gods are crowned in the city; their flowers have broken your rods;
They are merciful, clothed with pity, the young compassionate gods,
But for me their new device is barren, the days are bare;
Things long past over suffice, and men forgotten that were.
Time and the gods are at strife; ye dwell in the midst thereof,
Draining a little life from the barren breasts of love.
I say to you, cease, take rest: yea, I say to you all, be at peace,
Till the bitter milk of her breast and the barren bosom shall cease.
Wilt thou yet take all, Galilean? But these thou shalt not take—
The laurel, the palms, and the paean, the breasts of the nymphs
    in the brake,
Breasts more soft than a dove's, that trembled with tenderer breath;
And all the wings of the Loves, and all the joy before death;
All the feet of the hours that sound as a single lyre,
Dropped and deep in the flowers, with strings that flicker like fire.
More than these wilt thou give, things fairer than all these things?
nay, for a little we live, and life hath mutable wings.
A little while and we die; shall life not thrive as it may?
For no man under the sky lives twice, outliving his day,
And grief is a grievous thing, and a man hath enough of his tears;
Why should he labor, and bring fresh grief to blacken his years?

Thou hast conquered, O pale Galilean; the world has grown gray
    from thy breath;
We have drunken of things Lethean, and fed on the fullness of death.
Laurel is green for a season, and love is sweet for a day;
But love grows bitter with treason, and laurel outlives not May.
Sleep, shall we sleep after all? for the world is not sweet in the end;
For the old faiths loosen and fall, the new years ruin and rend.
Fate is a sea without shore, and the soul is a rock that abides;
But the ears are vexed with the roar, and her face with the foam
    of the tides.
O lips that the live blood faints in, the leavings of racks and rods!
O ghastly stories of saints, dead limbs of gibbeted gods!
Though all men abase them before you in spirit, and all knees bend,
O kneel not, neither adore you, but standing look to the end.

All delicate days and pleasant, all spirits and sorrows are cast
Far out with the foam of the present that sweeps to the surf of the past;

Where beyond the extreme sea wall, and between the remote sea gates,
Waste water washes, and tall ships founder, and deep death waits;
Where, mighty with deepening sides, clad about with the seas as with wings,
And impelled of invisible tides, and fulfilled of unspeakable things,
White-eyed and poisonous-finned, shark-toothed and serpentine-curled,
Rolls, under the whitening wind of the future, the wave of the world.
The depths stand naked in sunder behind it, the storms flee away;
In the hollow before it the thunder is taken and snared as a prey;
In its sides is the north wind bound; and its salt is of all men's tears,
With light of ruin, and sound of changes, and pulse of years;
With travail of day after day, and with trouble of hour upon hour.
And bitter as blood is the spray; and the crests are as fangs that devour;
And its vapor and storm of its steam as the sighing of spirits to be;
And its noise as the noise in a dream; and its depths as the roots of the sea;
And the height of its heads as the height of the utmost stars of the air;
And the ends of the earth at the might thereof tremble, and time is made bare.
Will ye bridle the deep sea with reins, will ye chasten the high sea with rods?
Will ye take her to chain her with chains, who is older than all ye gods?
All ye as a wind shall go by, as a fire shall ye pass and be past;
Ye are gods, and behold ye shall die, and the waves be upon you at last.
In the darkness of time, in the deeps of the years, in the changes of things,
Ye shall sleep as a slain man sleeps, and the world shall forget you or kings.
Though the feet of thine high priest tread where thy lords and our
        forefathers trod,
Though these that were gods are dead, and being dead art a god,
Though before thee the throned Cytherean be fallen, and hidden her head,
Yet thy kingdom shall pass, Galilean, thy dead shall go down to thee dead.

* * *

[INVOCATION TO PROSERPINA]

Thou art more than the gods who number the days of our temporal breath;
For these give labor and slumber; but thou, Proserpina, death.
Therefore now at thy feet I abide for a season in silence. I know
I shall die as my fathers died, and sleep as they sleep; even so.
For the glass of the years is brittle wherein we gaze for a span.
A little soul for a little bears up this corpse which is man.
So long I endure, no longer; and laugh not again, neither weep.
For there is no god found stronger than death; and death is a sleep.

(1866)

The Garden of Proserpine

Here, where the world is quiet,
    Here, where all trouble seems
Dead winds' and spent waves' riot
    In doubtful dreams of dreams.
I watch the green field growing
For reaping folk and sowing,
For harvest-time and mowing,
    A sleepy world of streams.
I am tired of tears and laughter,
    And men that laugh and weep;
Of what may come hereafter
    For men that sow to reap:
I am weary of days and hours,
Blown buds of barren flowers,
Desires and dreams and powers
    And everything but sleep.

Here life has death for neighbor,
    And far from eye or ear
Wan waves and wet winds labor,
    Weak ships and spirits steer,
They drive adrift, and whither
They wot not who make thither;
But no such winds blow hither,
    And no such things grow here,

No growth of moor or coppice,
    No heather-flower or vine,
But bloomless buds of poppies,
    Green grapes of Proserpine,
Pale beds of blowing rushes
Where no leaf blooms or blushes
Save this whereof she crushes
    For dead men deadly wine.

Pale, without name or number,
    In fruitless fields of corn,
They bow themselves and slumber
    All night till light is born;

And like a soul belated,
In hell and heaven unmated,
By cloud and mist abated
    Comes out of darkness morn.

Though one were strong as seven,
    He too with death shall dwell,
Nor wake with wings in heaven,
    Nor weep for pains in hell;
Though one were fair as roses,
His beauty clouds and closes,
And well though love reposes,
    In the end it is not well.

Pale, beyond porch and portal,
    Crowned with calm leaves, she stands
Who gathers all things mortal
    With cold immortal hands;
Her languid lips are sweeter
Than love's who fears to greet her
To men that mix and meet her
    From many times and lands.

She waits for each and other,
    She waits for all men born;
Forgets the earth her mother,
    The life of fruits and corn;
And spring and seed and swallow
Take wing for her and follow
Where summer song rings hollow
    And flowers are put to scorn.

There go the loves that wither,
    The old loves with wearier wings;
And all dead years draw thither,
    And all disastrous things;
Dead dreams of days forsaken,
Blind buds that snows have shaken,
Wild leaves that winds have taken,
    Red strays of ruined springs.

We are not sure of sorrow,
    And joy was never sure;
Today will die tomorrow;
    Time stoops to no man's lure;
And love, grown faint and fretful,
With lips but half regretful
Sighs, and with eyes forgetful
    Weeps that no loves endure.

From too much love of living,
    From hope and fear set free,
We thank with brief thanksgiving
    Whatever gods may be
That no life lives for ever;
That dead men rise up never;
That even the weariest river
    Winds somewhere safe to sea.

Then star nor sun shall waken,
    Nor any change of light
Nor sound of waters shaken,
    Nor any sound or sight;
Nor wintry leaves nor vernal,
Nor days nor things diurnal;
Only the sleep eternal
    In an eternal night.

                                (1866)

FROM "AVE ATQUE VALE" (IN MEMORY OF CHARLES BAUDELAIRE)

4

O sleepless heart and somber soul unsleeping,
    That were athirst for sleep and no more life
    And no more love, for peace and no more strife!
Now the dim gods of death have in thy keeping
    Spirit and body and all the springs of song,
    Is it well where love can do no wrong,
Where stingless pleasure has no foam or fang
    Behind the unopening closure of her lips?

Is it not well where soul from body slips
And flesh from bone divides without a pang
 As dew from flower-bell drips?

5

It is enough; the end and the beginning
 Are one thing to thee, who art past the end.
 O hand unclasped of unbeholden friend,
For thee no fruits to pluck, no palms for winning,
 No triumph and no labor and no lust,
 Only dead yew-leaves and a little dust,
O quiet eyes wherein the light saith naught,
 Whereto the day is dumb, nor any night
 With obscure finger silences your sight,
Nor in your speech the sudden soul speaks thought,
 Sleep, and have sleep for light.

(1868)

THOMAS HARDY (1840–1928)

Hardy, whom Americans know mainly as a novelist, was also an important poet and an unwavering mortalist. His poems have an unmistakable rough-hewn quality; they are a dark, grieving, regretful view of the human condition. The fact that, as Hardy says in "Hap," he doesn't even have a deity or demon to blame for his suffering only makes things worse. His first poem is an epitaph for a simple British soldier killed in the Boer War; and his work in general is filled with laments for the dead, sometimes grandly tragic, as in his "Convergence of the Twain," about the sinking of the *Titanic*, sometimes quietly mournful, sometimes even quirkily comical, as in "Ah, Are You Digging on My Grave?"

DRUMMER HODGE

1

They throw in Drummer Hodge, to rest
    Uncoffined—just as found:
His landmark is a kopje-crest*
    That breaks the veldt around;
And foreign constellations west
    Each night above his mound.

2

Young Hodge the Drummer never knew—
    Fresh from his Wessex home—
The meaning of the broad Karoo,†
    The Bush, the dusty loam,
And why uprose to nightly view
    Strange stars amid the gloam.

---

*small hill
†arid plateau

3

Yet portion of this unknown plain
　　Will Hodge forever be;
His homely Northern breast and brain
　　Grown to some southern tree,
And strange-eyed constellations reign
　　Hides stars eternally.

(1902)

SHE HEARS THE STORM

There was a time in former years—
　　While my roof-tree was his—
When I should have been distressed by fears
　　At such a night as this.

I should have murmured anxiously,
　　"The pricking rain strikes cold;
His road is bare of hedge or tree,
　　And he is getting old."

But now the fitful chimney-roar,
　　The drone of Thornecombe trees,
The Froom in flood upon the moor,
　　The mud of Mellstock Leaze.

The candle slanting sooty-wick'd,
　　Yet thuds upon the thatch,
The eave-drops on the window flicked,
　　The clacking garden-hatch,

And what they mean to wayfarers,
　　I scarcely heed or mind;
He has won that storm-tight roof of hers
　　Which Earth grants all her kind.

(1909)

AH, ARE YOU DIGGING ON MY GRAVE?

"Ah, are you digging on my grave
    My loved one?—planting rue?"
—"No: yesterday he went to wed
One of the brightest wealth has bred.
'It cannot hurt her now,' he said.
    'That I should not be true.'"

"Then who is digging on my grave?
    My nearest dearest kin?"
—"Ah, no; they sit and think, "What use?
What good will planting flowers produce?
No tendance of her mound can loose
    Her spirit from Death's gin*.'"

"But some one digs upon my grave?
    My enemy?—prodding sly?"
—"Nay: when she heard you had passed the Gate
That shuts on all flesh soon or late,
She thought you no more worth her hate,
    And cares not where you lie."

"Then, who is digging on my grave?
    Say—since I have not guessed!"
—"O it is I, my mistress dear,
Your little dog, who still lives near,
And much I hope my movements here
    Have not disturbed your rest?"

"Ah, yes! *You* dig upon my grave . . .
    Why flashed it not on me
That one true heart was left behind!
What feeling do we ever find
To equal among human kind
    A dog's fidelity!"

"Mistress, I dug upon your grave
    To bury a bone in case

---

*trap

I should be hungry near this spot
When passing on my daily trot.
I am sorry, but I quite forgot
    It was your resting place.

(1914)

AFTERWARDS

When the Present has latched its postern behind my tremulous stay
    And the May month flaps its glad green leaves like wings,
Delicate-filmed as new-spun silk, will the neighbours say.
    "He was a man who used to notice such things"?

If it be in the dusk when, like an eyelid's soundless blink,
    The dewfall-hawk comes crossing the shades to alight
Upon the wind-warped upland thorn, a gazer may think,
    "To him this must have been a familiar sight."

If I pass during some nocturnal blackness, mothy and warm,
    When the hedgehog travels furtively over the lawn,
One may say, "He strove that such innocent creatures should come
        to no harm,
    But he could do little for them; and now he is gone."

If, when hearing that I have been stilled at last, they stand at the door,
    Watching the full-starred heavens that winter sees,
Will this thought rise on those who will meet my face no more,
    "He was one who had an eye for such mysteries"?
    And will any say when my bell of quittance is heard in the gloom,
    And a crossing breeze cuts a pause in its outrollings,
Till they rise again, as they were a new bell's boom,
    "He hears it not now, but used to notice such things"?

(1917)

WILLIAM JAMES (1842–1910) AND BERTRAND RUSSELL (1872–1970)

O f these two philosophers, who shared a fine prose style and broad popular appeal, James was an agnostic, whereas Russell was a wholehearted mortalist. But in two brief passages both writers forcefully confront the issue of *cosmic* mortalism, that is: what are we to make of the prospect not just of individual death but of the eventual disappearance of the entire human race?

WILLIAM JAMES,
FROM *THE VARIETIES OF RELIGIOUS EXPERIENCE* (1902)

The lustre of the present hour is always borrowed from the background of possibilities it goes with. Let our common experiences be enveloped in an eternal moral order; let our suffering have an immortal significance; let Heaven smile upon the earth, and deities pay their visits; let faith and hope be the atmosphere which man breathes in;—and his days pass by with zest; they stir with prospects, they thrill with remoter values. Place round them on the contrary the curdling cold and gloom and absence of all permanent meaning which for pure naturalism and the popular science evolutionism of our time are all that is visible ultimately, and the thrill stops short, or turns rather to an anxious trembling.

For naturalism, fed on recent cosmological speculations, mankind is in a position similar to that of a set of people living on a frozen lake, surrounded by cliffs over which there is no escape, yet knowing that little by little the ice is melting, and the inevitable day drawing near when the last film of it will disappear, and to be drowned ignominiously will be the human creature's portion. The merrier the skating,the warmer and more sparkling the sun by day, and the ruddier the bonfires at night, the more poignant the sadness with which one must take in the meaning of the total situation.

BERTRAND RUSSELL, FROM *MYSTICISM AND LOGIC* (1947)

That man is the product of causes which had no prevision of the end they were achieving; that his origin, his growth, his hopes and fears, his loves and his beliefs, are but the outcome of accidental collocations of atoms; that no fire, no heroism, no intensity of thought and feeling can preserve an individual life beyond the grave, that all the labours of all the ages, all the devotion, all the inspiration, all the noonday brightness of human genius are destined to extinction in the vast death of the solar system, and that the whole temple of man's achievement must inevitably be buried beneath the debris of a universe in ruins—all these things, if not quite beyond dispute, are yet so nearly certain that no philosophy which rejects them can hope to stand.

FRIEDRICH NIETZSCHE (1844–1900)

Though a fierce atheist and a resolute mortalist, Nietzsche was not all that interested in death. After brilliantly evoking, in *The Gay Science* (see the first excerpt below), the way humans deny and ignore death, he concludes: "It makes me happy to see how people stubbornly refuse to think the thought of death. I would very much like to do something to make the thought of life a hundred times *more worth thinking about* for them" (278). Nevertheless, Nietzsche does provide some grad mortalist perspectives: for him the denial of all metaphysical visions of personal survival in the afterlife (and, more broadly, the rejection of all sentimental anthropocentrism) is a necessary first step to honest thinking and living.

The thought of death.—It gives me a melancholy happiness to live amid this maze of little streets, of needs and voices: how much enjoyment, impatience, and desire, how much thirsty life and drunken life comes to light there every moment! It is always like the scene at the last moment before the departure of a ship full of emigrants: people have more to say to one another than ever, time presses; the ocean with its desolate silence is waiting impatiently behind all the noise—so greedy and certain of its prey. Yet all of them think that what happened before is little or nothing, while the near future is everything. And hence this bustle, this shouting, this vying to drown out and push ahead of everyone else. Everyone wants to be first in this future—and yet death and the silence of death are the only things certain and shared by all in this future. How strange that this, the only certainty and commonality, makes practially no impression on people, and that the last thing they feel is their brotherhood in death.

The Gay Science, 278

The new basic feeling: our definitive fleetingness.—It used to be, the feeling of human grandeur of man was sought for by pointing to our divine *origin*: this has now become a forbidden path, because at its gate stands the ape, along with other hideous creatures, and sympathetically bares its teeth, as if to say: Go no further in this direction! So now people try going in opposite direction: the path *whither* the human race is headed is supposed to serve as proof of its splendor and kin-ship with God. Ah, this too is a dead end! At the end of this path stands the funeral urn of the *last* human being and gravedigger (with the inscription "*nihil humani a me alienum puto*" [I think nothing human is alien to me]). However high the human race may have evolved—and perhaps in the end it will stand even lower than it did in the beginning! there is no overpass into a higher order, any more than the ant and the earwig at the end of their "earthly course" will ascend to kinship with God and eternity. What is to be drags behind it what has been: why should an exception be made in this eternal spectacle for some little planet and some little species on it. Away with such sentimentalities.

Daybreak, 49

Let us be on guard!—Let us be on guard against thinking that the world is a living being. Whither is it supposed to expand? What is it supposed to feed on/ How could it grow and multiply? We do have a rough idea of what the organic is: and we're supposed to take the unspeakably derivative, late, rare, and accidental features that we perceive only on the surface of the earth, and reinterpret them as something essential, universal, eternal, in the manner of those who call the universe an organism? That disgusts me. Let us be on guard against believing the universe is a machine: it was certainly not built with any goal in mind. We do it far too high an honor with the word "machine." . . . The astral order in which we live is an excep-tion; this order and the relative permanence that depends upon it have once again made possible the exception of exceptions: the formation of the organic. By con-trast, the overall character of the world is, for all eternity, chaos, not in the sense of a lack of necessity, but of a lack of order, structure, form, beauty, wisdom and whatever else we call all our aesthetic human qualities. Judged from the standpoint of our reason, the failed throws of the dice are far and away the rule; the exceptions are not the secret goal, and the whol "music box" eternally repeats its tune, which can never be called a melody—and ultimately even the phrase "failed throw" is already a humanization with an implied reproach. But how could we dare to blame or praise the universe! let us be on guard against attributing to it heartlessness or reason or their opposites: it is neither perfect, nor beautiful, nor noble, and has no desire to become any of those things; it is most certainly not striving to imitate humans! It also has no dirve for self-preservation—actually, it has no dirves of any sort. Let us be on guard against saying that there are laws in nature. There are only necessities: there is no one to command, no one to obey, no one to transtgress. If you know that there are no goals, then you know that there is no chance either: for only in the neighborhood of a world of purposes does the word "chance" make sense. Let us be on guard against saying that death is the opposite of life. The living being is only a species of the death, and a very rare species at that.

The Gay Science, 109

The "after death."—Christianity found the notion of infernal punishment all over the whole Roman Empire: the numerous secret cults had brooded over the idea with particular satisfaction as the most fruitful egg of their power. Epicurus thought he could do nothing greater for his fellow humans than tear out the roots of *this* belief. His triumph, which rings and fades away most beautifully in the mouth of his gloomy and yet enlightened disciple, the Roman Lucretius, came too early. Christianity took the belief in subterranean terrors, which was already fading, under its special protection; and how clever it was to do so. Otherwise without this bold dipping into out-and-out paganism, how could it have conquered the popular cults of Mithra and Isis? So it won over the fearful—the strongest adherents of a new faith! The Jews, as a people that has always clung to life—like the Greeks and more than the Greeks—had done little to cultivate these ideas: eternal death as the punishment for the sinner, and no chance of resurrection as the supreme threat. That was already menace enough for these peculiar people, who had no wish to get rid of their bodies but, with their sophisicated Egyptianism, hoped to save them for all eternity. (The Jewish martyr whom we read about in the Second Book of Mac-cabees [2 Macc. 7.7–9—ed.] had no intention of relinquishing his ripped-out intes-tines: he wanted to *have* them at the resurrection—that makes the story Jewish!)

For the first Christians the thought of eternal tortures was utterly remote: they felt they were *redeemed* "from death" and from day to day expected a transforma-tion, with no more death. How strange the first case of a death among these expec-tant people must have been. What a mixture of astonishment, rejoicing, doubt, shame, and fervor—truly a reproof to great artists!) Paul couldn't come up with anything better to say about his Redeemer than that he had *opened* the gateway of immortality to everyone—he did not yet believe in the resurrection of the unre-deemed. Indeed, as a result of his teachings on the impossibility of fulfilling the law and on death as the consequence of sin, he suspected that in principle no one had ever become immortal (or very few—and then only thanks to unmerited grace). Only now was immortality *beginning* to open its doors—and ultimately it too was reserved to very few people, as the arrogance of the elect can't resist adding.

In other places, where the instinct for life was not as great as it was among Jews and Jewish Christians, and where the prospect of immortality didn't neces-sarily seem better than the prospect of permanent death, the pagan and yet not altogether un-Jewish addition of Hell proved a welcome tool in the hands of the missionaries. A new doctrine arose that the unredeemed sinner was immortal too: the doctrine of the eternally damned; and it was more powerful than the fast-fading notion of *permanent death*. It is only *science* that has had to recapture that notion, as it did by rejecting at once every other idea of death and every life in the Beyond. We are the poorer for one interest we have lost: the "afterdeath" no longer concerns us. This is an unspeakable benefit, but still too new to be per-ceived as such far and wide.—And Epicurus triumphs all over again!

Daybreak, 72

On the torments of the soul.—Whenever a person inflicts torments on someone else's body, everyone now raises a loud outcry. The indignation against anyone capable of such a thing bursts out immediately. Indeed, we tremble when we merely imagine a torment being visited on a human or animal; and we find it quite unbearable simply to hear about a solidly documented case of this sort.

But we are still a long way having the same widespread and emphatic feelings about the torments of the soul and the horror of inflicting them. Christianity has made use of them to an unheard-of degree and still continues to preach this kind of torture. In fact, it complains quite innocently about backsliding and lukewarmness when it comes across a situation lacking such torments. The result of all this is that the human race nowadays is still showing the same timid patience and indecisiveness as before toward cruelty against the bodies of humans and animals. . . .

Plutarch gives a dismal picture of the condition of a superstitious person in the pagan world: this picture looks very tame next to the medieval Christian who *conjectures* that he may not be able to escape "eternal torment" any longer. Frightful omens appear to him: perhaps a stork holding a snake in its beak and still *hesitating* to swallow it. Or nature suddenly turns pale, or blazing colors fly across the landscape. Or the figures of dead relatives approach, their faces marked by fearful sufferings. Or the dark walls of the sleeping sinner's room grow bright, and on them appear instruments of torture in a thick yellow smoke and a tangled mass of snakes and devils. Indeed, what a horrible place Christianity had already managed to turn the earth into when it set up crucifixes everywhere and thus defined the earth as the place "where the just man is *tortured* to death"! And when the power of the great preachers of penance drove out into the open all the hidden suffering of the individual, the torments of the "little chamber": when, for example, a George Whitfield (1714–1770), preached "like a dying man to the dying," now violently weeping, now stamping loudly and passionately, in the most sudden and piercing tones, and without hesitation aimed the whole weight of his attack upon some individual in the audience and in a terrifying manner singled him out from the community—how the earth really did seem to want to transform itself each time into the "Valley of the Shadow of Death"! Whole crowds of people who had poured together seemed to have been fallen prey to a madness; many were convulsed with fear; others lay unconscious and motionless; some trembled violently or rent the air with piercing cries that went on for hours. Everywhere there was loud breathing as if people were half choked and gasping for breath. "And truly," an eye-witness of one such sermon tells us, "almost all the sounds to be heard were those of people *who were lying in bitter torment.*"—Let us never forget that Christianity was the first to make the *death-bed* a bed of torture, and that with the scenes that have since then been played out upon it, with the horrible tones which could he heard here for the first time, the senses and the blood of countless witnesses were poisoned for life and for the life of their posterity. Imagine a harmless human being who can't get over having heard such words as these: "Oh eternity! Oh that I had no soul! O that I had never been born! I am damned, damned, lost for ever. Six days ago you could have helped me, but that time is past. Now I belong to the Devil. I will go with him to Hell. Break, break, poor hearts of stone! Will you not break? What more can be done for hearts of stone? I am damned that you may be saved! There he is! Yes, there he is! Come, good Devil! Come!"

Daybreak, 79

To the dreamers of immortality.—So you want *eternal* duration for your beautiful self-consciousness? Isn't that shameless? Don't you have a thought for all the other things that would then have to *put up with you* for all eternity, as they have hitherto endured you with a more than Christian patience? Or do you think you can supply them with an eternal sense of well-being in your presence? A single immortal human being on earth would be enough to throw everything else that was still there into a universal suicidal fit out of *antipathy to him*. And you earth-dwellers, with your paltry notions of a few thousand little minutes, you want to unload your eternal plague on eternal universal existence. Talk about pushiness!—Well, after all, let's be kind to a creature who lasts only seventy years—he hasn't been able to exercise his imagination enough in sketching out what his own "eternal boredom" would be like—he just hasn't had the time!

Daybreak, 211

If one shifts life's center of gravity out of life into the "Beyond"—into *nothingness*—one has simply robbed life of its center of gravity. The great lie of personal immortality destroys all reason, all nature in the instincts—everything beneficial, everything life-promoting, everything that guarantees the future in the instincts now excites mistrust. To live in such a way that life no longer has any meaning now becomes the "meaning" of life.—What is the point of public spirit, what is the point of gratitude for one's lineage and ancestors, why cooperate, why trust, why promote and aim for the common good?—They are all so many "temptations," so many diversions from the "right road"—"*one thing* is necessary" . . . that everyone, as an "immortal soul," holds the same rank as everyone else, that in the totality of all beings the "salvation" of *every* individual can lay claim to eternal importance; that is, bigots and three-quarter-lunatics are free to imagine that for their sake the laws of nature will be constantly *broken*—that sort of heightening of egoism to infinity, to utter shamelessness, cannot be branded with sufficient contempt. . . .

"Salvation of the soul"—baldly put: "The world revolves around *me*."—The poison of the doctrine "*equal* rights for all"—Christianity has disseminated this as its most basic principle. Operating out of the most secret crannies of bad instincts, Christianity has waged a war to the death against every feeling of reverence and distance between individuals, which is the prerequisite for every heightening, for every growth in culture. Out of the resentment of the masses it has forged its *chief weapon* against *us*, against everything noble, joyful, highhearted on earth, against our happiness on earth.—The "immortality" conceded to every Peter and Paul has been to date the greatest and most vicious assassination attempt ever made on *noble* humanity.

The Antichrist, 43

(trans. Peter Heinegg)

SIGMUND FREUD (1856–1939)

One of the great modern patriarchs of unbelief, Freud attacks religion in *The Future of an Illusion* (1927) as a childish vestige of primitive society. Freud doesn't argue his case so much as he trumpets it, flatly asserting that religion arose out of an attempt to conciliate the implacable anthropomorphized forces of nature by deifying and praying to them. For Freud, the enlightened modern individual must simply accept the world as it is (once science has done its utmost to carve a habitable clearing in the jungle, so to speak), including the prospect of permanent death.

FROM *THE FUTURE OF AN ILLUSION*

But how ungrateful, how thoroughly short-sighted to strive to abolish civilization. In that case the only thing left over would be the state of nature, which would be much harder to bear. True, nature would not demand from us any restrictions on our desires; she would let us indulge in them, but she has a peculiarly effective way of reining us in: she kills us, coldly, cruelly, and ruthlessly (as it seems to us), in some cases precisely by the means of our satisfaction. After all, it is because of these very dangers that nature threatens us with that we have gotten together and created civilization, which, among other things, is supposed to make possible our life in common. Civilization's main task, in fact, its actual *raison d'être* is to defend us against nature.

Everyone knows that in some ways it already succeeds reasonably well at this; and evidently it will do so even better in the future. But no one is deluded enough to believe that nature has already been conquered; and few dare to hope that one day she will be wholly subject to humans. There are the elements, which seem to mock every human effort to master them: the earth, which trembles, tears to shreds, and buries humans and all their works; the waters, which are churned up, overflowing and drowning everything; storms, which blast everything away. There are diseases, which we have just recently recognized as assaults by other living creatures. Finally there is the painful riddle of death, for which no remedy has yet been found, and probably never will be. Nature rises against us with these mighty powers, magnificent, cruel, inexorable; she rudely reminds us of our weakness and helplessness, which we thought we could evade through the work of civilization.

* * *

The gods are left with their threefold task: to ward off the terrors of nature, to reconcile us to the cruelty of fate, especially as shown in death, and to compensate us for the sufferings and deprivations imposed on the human race by civilized life in common.

* * *

So I have to contradict you [Freud's imaginary interlocutor, an entrenched traditionalist] when you go on to conclude that human beings simply cannot do without the consolation of the religious illusion, that without it they would be able to bear the heavy burdens of life and cruel reality. That would be true, to be sure, of those down whose throat you have been pouring, ever since childhood, sweet—or bitter-sweet—poison. But what about the others, who have been raised soberly? Perhaps those who don't suffer from the neurosis won't need an intoxicant to deaden the pain. Admittedly, humans will then find themselves in a difficult situation. They will have to admit their utter helplessness, their insignificance in the grand scheme of the world, no longer the center of creation, no longer the object of tender care from a kindly Providence. They will be in the same situation as a child who has left his father's house where he was so warm and comfortable. But isn't infantilism something we have to overcome? Humans can't remain children forever; eventually they have to go out into the cold, cruel world. This might be called "education for reality." Do I have to tell you that the only purpose of this piece is to call attention to the necessity of this step forward?

You are probably afraid that they won't pass this hard test. Well, we can always hope. It is already makes a difference when we know we have to rely on our own efforts: then we learn then to make proper use of them. Human beings are not entirely helpless. Since the days of the Flood their science has taught them a great deal, and it will extend their power still farther. And, as for the great necessities of Fate, which nothing can help, they will learn to bear them with resignation. What good to them is the pretence that they own a grand estate on the moon, which has yet to yield a penny of profit? As honest small farmers on this earth they will know how to cultivate their little patch of ground so that it supports them [cf. Voltaire's *Candide*, "We must cultivate our garden"—ed.]. By withdrawing their expectations from the Beyond and concentrating all their freed-up powers on earthly life, they will probably manage to make a life that is tolerable for everyone and a civilization that oppresses no one. Then they will be able to join one of our fellow-unbelievers [Heinrich Heine] in saying with no regrets:

> *Den Himmel überlassen wir*   We leave heaven
> *Den Engeln und den Spatzen.* To the angels and the sparrows.

(trans. Peter Heinegg)

GEORGE SANTAYANA
(1863–1952)

B orn in Madrid, a professor of philosophy (at Harvard, from 1889 to 1912) who spent the last forty years of his life in Europe and died in a convent in Rome, Santayana was a gentle, retiring mortalist whose views may be summed up in his bon mot, "There is no cure for birth and death save to enjoy the interval" (*Soliloquies in England*).

FROM *THREE PHILOSOPHICAL POETS*

Dying is something ghastly, as being born is something ridiculous; and, even if no pain were involved in quitting or entering this world, we might still say what Dante's Francesca says of it: *Il modo ancor m'offende,*—"I shudder at the way of it." If the fear of death were merely the fear of dying, it would be better dealt with by medicine than by argument. There is, or there might be, an art of dying well, of dying painlessly, willingly, and in season,—as in those noble partings which Attic gravestones depict,—especially if we were allowed to choose our own time.

But the radical fear of death, I venture to think, is something quite different. It is the love of life. It is something antecedent and spontaneous. It teaches every animal to seek its food and its mate, and to protect its offspring; as also to resist or fly from all injury to the body, and most of all from threatened death. It is the original impulse by which good is discriminated from evil, and hope from fear.

Nothing could be more futile, therefore, than to marshal arguments against that fear of death which is merely another name for the energy of life, or the tendency to self-preservation. What is most dreaded is not the agony of dying, nor yet the strange impossibility than when we do not exist we should suffer for not existing. What is dreaded is the defeat of a present will directed upon life and its various undertakings. Such a present will cannot be argued away, but it may be weakened by contradictions arising within it, by the irony of experience, or by ascetic discipline. To introduce ascetic discipline, to bring out the irony of experience, to expose the self-contradictions of the will, would be the true means of mitigating the love of life; and if the love of life were extinguished, the fear of death, like smoke arising from that fire, would have vanished also.

(1910)

MIGUEL DE UNAMUNO
(1864-1936)

There are few more poignant voices of mortalism than Miguel de Unamuno's. The Spanish (Basque) philosopher and writer was, in principle, a doubting believer, affirming his hope in immortality against all odds. But, as the following section from *The Tragic Sense of Life* (1913) makes clear, Unamuno's faith was a blind thrust of the will: his reason made it agonizingly clear to him what shaky ground he was standing on. It is easy to fault his logic, but hard not to sympathize with his predicament.

FROM *THE TRAGIC SENSE OF LIFE,* CHAPTER 3, "THE HUNGER FOR IMMORTALITY"

Let's dwell on this point about the immortal longing for immortality, even though the gnostics or intellectuals may say that what follows is rhetoric and not philosophy. Even the divine Plato, when he discoursed in the *Phaedo* about the immortality of the soul, said that it was appropriate to make up myths about it, *mythologein.*

Before all else, let's recall one more time—and it won't be the last—what Spinoza said about every being striving to persevere in itself. He wrote that this striving was its actual essence, which implies indefinite time; and that the soul finally, both in its clear and distinct ideas and in its confused ones, tends to persevere in its being with indefinite duration, and it's aware of this effort (*Ethice,* pars III, propositions VI–IX).

It's impossible for us, in fact, to conceive of ourselves as not existing, without some force being exerted that's great enough for consciousness to realize absolute unconsciousness, its own annihilation. Try, reader, to imagine yourself while wide awake what might be the state of your soul in deep sleep; try to fill your consciousness with a representation of unconsciousness, and you'll see. It causes the most anguished vertigo to persist in understanding it. We can't conceive ourselves as not existing,

The visible universe, which is the offspring of the instinct of conservation seems straitened to me; it's like a cage that feels too small, and against its bars my soul spins around; I need air to breathe. More, each time more; I want to be myself, and without ceasing to be that, to be the others as well, to incorporate into myself the totality of things visible and invisible, to extend myself to the unlimited reach of space, and to prolong myself to the endless point of time. Not to be it all and for ever is as if I didn't exist; and at least to be all myself, and to be it forever and forever. All or nothing!

All or nothing! And what other sense could "To be or not to be" have? This from the same poet who had Menenius say of Coriolanus (V.4.25) "he wants nothing of a god but eternity." Eternity! Eternity! That's the longing; the thirst for eternity is what is called love among men, and anyone who loves another want to become eternal in him. What's not eternal isn't real either.

Cries from the entrails of the soul have torn from the poets of all times this tremendous vision of the flowing of the waves of life, from Pindar's dream of a shadow (*skias onar*) to Calderón's "life is a dream" to Shakespeare's "We are such stuff / That dreams are made on." And this last line is more tragic than the Spaniard's, because while Calderón just says that our life is a dream, not we ourselves who dream it. Shakespeare makes *us* a dream, a dream that dreams.

* * *

Everything passes! Such is the refrain of all those who have pressed their mouth to and drunk from the gushing fountain of life, of all who have tasted the fruit of the Tree of the Knowledge of Good and Evil.

To be, to be forever, to be without end! The thirst to be, the thirst to be more! The hunger for God! The thirst for love that is eternal and makes us eternal! To be forever! To be God!

"You shall be as gods!" Genesis tells us (3.5) is what the serpent said to the first pair of lovers. "If in this life only we have hoped in Christ, we are of all men most to be pitied," writes the Apostle (1 Cor. 15.19). And all religion takes its start historically from the cult of the dead, that is to say, of immortality.

The tragic Portuguese Jew from Amsterdam wrote that the free man thinks of nothing less than of death. But that free man is a dead man, free from life's tensile spring, lacking in love, a slave of his freedom. The thought that I have to die and the enigma of what will happen afterwards is the very throb of my consciousness. When I contemplate the calm of greenery or the bright eyes through which a sister soul looks at mine, my consciousness swells; I feel the diastole of my soul, and I drench myself in the life all around me, and I believe in my own future. But just then the voice of the mystery whispers to me: "You will cease to be!" The wing of the Angel of Death brushes against me, and the systole of my soul floods the entrails of my spirit with the blood of divinity.

Like Pascal, I can't understand someone who claims that he doesn't give a farthing for business, and such carelessness "in a matter that concerns themselves, their eternity, their all, irritates me more than it touches me, it astonishes and terrifies me." And anyone who feels this way "is for me," as for Pascal, whose words I am quoting here, "a monster."

A thousand times and in a thousand tones it has been said that the cult of the dead ancestors is, as a rule, the starting point of primitive religions; and strictly speaking it's fair to say that what most sets humans apart from other animals is that in one way or another they keep their dead, never just handing them over to their thoughtless mother earth, who brings all things to birth. Humans are animals that guard their dead. Guarding them from what? From what do futile humans protect them? Poor little consciousness flees from its own annihilation; and, just like an animal spirit, thrust out from the womb of the world, it finds itself face with this, and knows how separate from the world it is, and it has to love a life different from that of the world itself. And so the earth would run the risk of being turned into a vast cemetery before the dead themselves die again.

When the living built nothing more for themselves than earthen huts or shacks of straw, which the harsh weather would destroy, barrows were heaped up for the dead; and stone was used for tombs before it was used for houses. The mighty houses of the dead have conquered the ages, not the houses of the living; not the places for sojourning but for staying forever.

This cult, not of death but of immortality, starts religions off and keeps them going. Amid the delirium of destruction, Robespierre had the Convention proclaim the existence of the Supreme Being and of "the consoling principle of the immortality of the soul"; and the fact is that the Incorruptible was terrified at the idea that his own body would one day would fall prey to corruption.

A disease? Perhaps. But anyone who disregards disease has no regard for health; and man is essentially and substantially a diseased animal. A disease? Perhaps it is, but then so is life itself, which holds it prisoner, and the only health possible, death. But this disease is the source of all-powerful health. From the depths of this anguish, from the abyss of the sense of our mortality, we make our way out into the light of another heaven, as Dante came forth from the depths of Hell to see the stars once more:

e quindi uscimmo a riveder le stelle. [*Inferno* xxxiv.139]

Though this meditation on our mortality may not at first cause anguish, in the end it doesn't strengthen us. Recollect yourself, reader, and imagine that you are slowly disintegrating, as your light is extinguished, as things around you go dumb and make no sound, wrapping you in silence; as the objects you handle melt between your fingers, as the floor slips from under your feet, as your memories blur and fade away, as everything dissipates into nothingness and you yourself dissipate, and you're not even left with the consciousness of nothingness for a shadow to lay hold of, in some fantastic fashion.

I once heard the story about a poor reaper who died in a hospital bed. When the priest came to anoint his hands as part of the last rites, the reaper refused to open his right hand, in which he was clutching some dirty coins, unaware that very soon his hand wouldn't be his and he wouldn't be himself. And so we close and clutch not our hands, but our heart, trying to clutch in it the whole world.

A friend once confessed to me that foreseeing—at a time when his physical health was in full vigor—that a violent death was near, he thought he could concentrate his life, living it in the few days he figured were left . . . by writing a book. Vanity of vanities!

If when the body dies on me, the body which sustains me and which I call mine, to distinguish it from myself, which is "I," if my consciousness returns to the absolute unconsciousness from which it sprouted, and if what happens to me happens to the consciousness of all my brothers and sisters in humanity, then our elaborate human lineage is nothing but an appalling procession of phantasms who march from nothingness to nothingness, and humanitarianism is the most inhuman thing known.

And the remedy is not the one proposed by the old folk song that says:

Every time that I think
I'm going to have to die,
I spread my coat down on the ground
And gorge on old shuteye.

No! The remedy is to look at it face to face, fixing out eyes on the eyes of the Sphinx, which is how to undo the evil spell lodged here with it.

If we all die altogether, what is it all for? It's the "what for?" of the Sphinx; it's the "What for?" that eats into the marrow of our soul; it's the progenitor of the anguish that makes us love hope.

Among the poetic complaints of the poor demented poet William Cowper (1731–1800) there are some lines written under the weight of delirium, where, feeling himself to be the target of divine vengeance he exclaims:

Hell might afford my miseries a shelter.

This is a Puritan sentiment, preoccupation with sin and predestination. But read these much more terrible words of Sénancour (1770–1846), so full of desperation—not the Protestant, but the Catholic variety—, when he has his Obermann say: "Man is born to perish . . . That may be; but let us perish resisting, and if nothingness is our fate, let us not make it a just fate." And I must in fact confess, painful as the confession may be, that in the days of the ingenuous faith of my youth, I never quaked with fear at the descriptions, horrifying as they were, of the tortures of Hell. I always felt that nothingness was far more frightening. Anyone who is suffering is alive, and anyone who lives in suffering loves and hopes, even though on the gate of his dwelling place they hang a sign saying "Abandon all hope!" And it's better to live in pain than to peacefully cease to exist. At bottom, I just couldn't believe in the atrocity of a Hell, of an eternity of punishment, nor did I see a truer Hell than nothingness and the prospect of it. And I continue to believe that if we all believed in our salvation from nothingness, we would all be better.

What is this acquired taste for life, *la joie de vivre*, that people talk to us about now? The hunger for God, the thirst for eternity, for survival, will always stifle in us that pathetic enjoyment of the life that passes and doesn't abide. It's the insatiable love of life, the love that wants life be unending, that most often thrusts us into the longing for death. "Once I am annihilated, if I *do* die completely—we tell ourselves—my world is finished, simply finished. And, if so, why not have it end as soon as possible, lest new consciousnesses come forth to suffer the sorrowful delusion of a passing and merely apparent existence? If, once the illusion of life is dispelled, living for the sake of life itself or for others who will have to die in their turn doesn't fill the soul, why bother living? Death is our remedy." And that's how laments are written about never-ending rest, out of fear of it, and death is called liberation.

Years ago, the poet of pain, of annihilation, Giacomo Leopardi, once he lost the ultimate delusion, that of thinking himself eternal,

Perì l'inganno estremo
ch'eterno io mi credei,

spoke to his heart about "the infinite vanity of everything." He saw that love and death were blood brothers, and that when "a loving affection, languid and weary, is born deep in the heart, along with it we feel in the breast a desire to die." With the majority of those who take their own lives, it's love that guides their arm, it's the supreme yearning for life, for more life, of prolonged and perpetual life that takes them to death, once they are persuaded that their yearning is in vain.

The problem is tragic and for ever, and the more we try to flee it, the more we crash into it. It was the serene (did I say serene?) Plato, twenty-four centuries ago, who in his dialogue on immortality of the soul let his own soul blurt out, when he was speaking of our doubtful daydream of being immortal and of the risk that it was in vain: "The risk is beautiful!"—*kalos gar ho kindynos*. It's a beautiful chance we can take that the soul may never die on us. This view was the seed of Pascal's famous argument about the "wager."

In the face of this risk, and in an attempt to suppress it, people give me logical proofs that belief in the immortality of the soul is absurd. But these ratiocinations don't affect me, because they're reasons and nothing but reasons; and the heart doesn't feed on reasons. I don't want to die, no. I don't want to, nor do I want to want to. I want to live forever, forever, forever, and to live as myself, this poor "I" that I am and that feels itself being here and now; and this is reason why the problem of the duration of my soul, of own soul, is such torture to me.

I am the center of my Universe, the center of the Universe, and in my supreme anguish I cry with Michelet: "My I! They are snatching my I!" For "What will it profit a man, if he gains the whole world and forfeits his life?" Mt. 16.26). Egoism, you say? There is nothing more universal than the individual, because the fate of one is the fate of all. Every man is worth more than all of Humanity, nor does it do any good to sacrifice each to all, except insofar as all sacrifice themselves to each one. What you call egoism is the principle of psychic gravity, the necessary postulate. "Love your neighbor as yourself," we were told, which presupposes that each man loves himself; and we weren't told: "Love yourself." And yet, we don't know how to love ourselves.

* * *

And they come along trying to deceive us with the deceit of deceits; they tell us that nothing is lost, that everything is transformed, altered, and changed, and not even the smallest bit of matter is annihilated, nor is the faintest jolt of energy totally dispersed. And there are people who expect us to be consoled with this. What a pathetic consolation! I'm not concerned about either my matter or my energy, since they aren't mine unless I myself am mine, that is, eternal. No, I don't yearn to drown in the great All, in infinite and eternal Matter or Energy, or in God; I don't want to be possessed by God, but to possess him, to become God without ceasing to be the "I" who is now telling you this. The swindles of monism are of no use to us. We want the bulk and heft, not the shadow, of eternity!

Materialism? Materialism, you say? No doubt, but either our spirit too is some kind of matter, or it is nothing. I tremble at the idea of having to tear myself away from my flesh. I tremble still more at the idea of having to tear myself away from everything sensible and material, from all substance. Perhaps this deserves the name of materialism, and if I cling to God with all my faculties and senses, it's so that He may take me in His arms beyond death, and looking me in the eye, with all his heavenly hosts, when the light in my eyes is going out forever. Am I deluding myself? Don't talk to me about delusion, just let me live!

They also call this pride—"stinking pride," Leopardi called it—and they ask us who we are, vile earthworms, to lay claim to immortality. "In the name of what? For what? By what right? In the name of what?" you ask. And in the name of what do we live? By what right do we exist? To exist is as gratuitous as to continue existing forever. Let's not talk about the name or the right or the wherefore of our yearning, which is an end in itself: because we will lose our reason in a whirlpool of absurdities. I don't claim any right or merit whatever; it's only a necessity: I need my yearning in order to live.

"And who are you?" you ask. And with Obermann I answer: "For the Universe, nothing; for myself, everything!" Pride? Pride to want to be immortal? Poor humans! A tragic destiny, no doubt, to have to base the affirmation of immortality on the restless and brittle rock of desire for immortality. But it would be great stupidity to condemn the yearning just because we believe it has been proved (without any such proof) that it can't he had. Am I dreaming. . . ? Let me dream. If this dream is my life, don't wake me up. I believe in the immortal origin of this yearning for immortality, which is the very substance of my soul. But do I really believe in it. . . ? And what do you want to be immortal for?" What for? Frankly I don't understand the question, because it's like asking the reason for reasons, the end of ends, the beginning of beginnings.

All these are things that can't be talked about.

(trans. Peter Heinegg)

MARCEL PROUST (1871–1922)

Proust is probably the supreme mortalist of twentieth-century literature (although it's hard to make excerpts from the intricate arabesques of his endlessly flowing narrative). His awareness that death ends everything is intensified and worsened by his (at times perhaps, nearly perverse) insistence that mutual love and meaningful communication are all but impossible, and that social life, which he so brilliantly chronicled, is a waste of time. The one solid value in Proust's world is art, which is (at least quasi-) permanent and knowable, unlike raw human experience. Art was the only believable religion; and, like other many other contemporary writers, he aspired to be its priest. Yet, though he spent the last fifteen years of his life toiling in eremitic isolation over his magnum opus, Proust was logically forced to admit, as he does here near the end of *Remembrance of Things Past*, that art too is mortal.

FROM *REMEMBRANCE OF THINGS PAST, TIME RECAPTURED*

This idea of death came to install itself for good in me the way a love affair does. Not that I loved death, I detested it. But, after having doubtless thought of it from time to time the way one thinks about a woman whom one does not yet love, the idea of death now adhered to the most profound level of my brain so totally that I couldn't occupy myself with anything without that thing first passing through the idea of death. And even if I didn't busy myself with anything, but remained in a state of complete repose, the idea of death kept me company as incessantly as the idea of myself. I don't think that on the day when I had become half-dead, it was the accidents that characterized that state—the impossibility of walking down a staircase, of remembering a name, of getting up—that had caused it, by a process of reasoning, even an unconscious one; but rather that it had come together, that inevitably the great mirror of the mind was reflecting a new reality. Still I didn't see how from the evils I had one could pass without warning to complete death. But then I thought of other people, of all those who die each day without the hiatus between their illness and their death striking us as extraordinary. I even thought that it was only because I saw them from the outside (still more than through the deceptions of hope) that certain maladies didn't strike me

159

as mortal, taken one by one, although I believed in my death, just as those who are the most persuaded that their end has come are nonetheless easily persuaded that if they cannot pronounce certain words, that has nothing to do with an attack or aphasia, etc., but comes from fatigue of the tongue or exhaustion following indigestion. . . .

No doubt my books too, like my fleshly being, would end up dying one day. But one must resign oneself to dying. One accepts the thought that in ten years time oneself, and in a hundred years one's books, will no longer exist. Eternal duration was never promised to works, any more than it was to men.

(trans. Peter Heinegg)

WALLACE STEVENS
(1879–1955)

Perhaps the only major poet who was also vice president of an insurance company, Stevens was a resolute mortalist, and in the complex musings of "Sunday Morning" he reflects, through a female persona who is pointedly staying away from church, on the fading of Christianity (or any otherworldly religion) and the paradoxical fact that death is "the mother of beauty," since it alone gives shape and intensity to the pleasures of this world.

SUNDAY MORNING

1

Complacencies of the peignoir, and late
Coffee and oranges in a sunny chair,
And the green freedom of a cockatoo
Upon a rug mingle to dissipate
The holy hush of ancient sacrifice.
She dreams a little, and she feels the dark
Encroachment of that old catastrophe,
As a calm darkens among water-lights.
The pungent oranges and bright, green wings
Seem things in some procession of the dead,
Winding across wide water, without sound.
The day is like wide water without sound,
Stilled for the passing of her dreaming feet
Over the seas, to silent Palestine,
Dominion of the blood and sepulcher.

2

Why should she give her bounty to the dead?
What is divinity if it can come

Only in silent shadows and in dreams?
Shall she not find in comforts of the sun,
In pungent fruit and bright, green wings, or else
In any balm or beauty of the earth,
Things to be cherished like the thought of heaven?
Divinity must live within herself:
Passions of rain, or moods in falling snow;
Grievings in loneliness, or unsubdued
Elations when the forest blooms; gusty
Emotions on wet roads on autumn nights;
All pleasures and all pains, remembering
The bough of summer and the winter branch.
These are the measures destined for her soul.

3

Jove in the clouds had his inhuman birth.
No mother suckled him, no sweet land gave
Large-mannered motions to his mythy mind.
He moved among us, as a muttering king,
Magnificent, would move among his hinds,*
Until our blood, commingling, virginal,
With heaven, brought such requital to desire
The very hinds discerned it, in a star,
Shall our blood fail? Or shall it come to be
The blood of paradise? And shall the earth
Seem all of paradise that we shall know?
The sky will be much friendlier then than now,
A part of labor and a part of pain,
And next to glory in enduring love,
Not this dividing and indifferent blue.

4

She says, "I am content when wakened birds,
Before they fly, test the reality
Of misty fields, by their sweet questionings;
But when the birds are gone, and their warm fields
Return no more, where, then, is paradise?"
There is not any haunt of prophecy,
Nor any old chimera of the grave,

---

*farm workers

Neither the golden underground, nor isle
Melodious, where spirits gat them home,
Nor visionary south, nor cloudy palm
Remote on heaven's hill, that has endured
As April's green endures, or will endure
Like her remembrance of awakened birds.
Or her desire for June and evening, tipped
By the consummation of the swallow's wings.

5

She says, "But in contentment I still feel
The need of some imperishable bliss."
Death is the mother of beauty; hence from her,
Alone, shall come fulfillment to our dreams
And our desires. Although she strews the leaves
Of sure obliteration on our paths,
The path sick sorrow took, the many paths,
Where triumph rang its brassy phrase, or love
Whispered a little out of tenderness,
She makes the willow shiver in the sun
For maidens who were wont to sit and gaze
Upon the grass, relinquished to their feet.
She causes boys to pile new plums and pears
On disregarded plate. The maidens taste
And stray impassioned in the littering leaves.

6

Is there no change or death in paradise?
Does ripe fruit never fail? Or do the boughs
Hang always heavy in that perfect sky,
Unchanging, yet so like our perishing earth,
With rivers like our own that seek for seas
They never find, the same receding shores
That never touch with inarticulate pang?
Why set the pear upon those river-banks
Or spice the shores with odors of the plum?
Alas, that they should wear out colors there,
The silken weavings of our afternoons,
And pick the strings of our insipid lutes!
Death is the mother of beauty, mystical,

Within whose burning bosom we devise
Our earthly mothers waiting, sleeplessly.

7

Supple and turbulent, a ring of men
Shall chant in orgy on a summer morn
Their boisterous devotion to the sun,
Not as a god, but as a god might be,
Naked among them, like a savage source.
Their chant shall be a chant of paradise,
Out of their blood, returning to the sky;
And in their chant shall enter, voice by voice,
The windy lake wherein their lord delights,
The trees, like serafin, and echoing hills,
That choir among themselves long afterward.
They shall know well the heavenly fellowship
Of men that perish and of summer morn.
And whence they came and whither they shall go
The dew upon their feet shall manifest.

8

She hears, upon that water without sound,
A voice that cries, "The tomb in Palestine
Is not the porch of spirits lingering.
It is the grave of Jesus, where he lay."
We live in an old chaos of the sun,
Or old dependence of day and night,
Or island solitude, unsponsored, free,
Of that wide water, inescapable.
Deer walk upon our mountains, and the quail
Whistle about is their spontaneous cries;
Sweet berries ripen in the wilderness;
And, in the isolation of the sky,
At evening, causal flocks of pigeons make
Ambiguous undulations as they sink
Downward to darkness, on extended wings.

(1923)

VIRGINIA WOOLF (1882–1941)

Virginia Woolf's life was as haunted by death as that of any major modern writer. The untimely deaths of her mother, Julia Stephen, her half-sister Stella, her brother Thoby, and her nephew Julian Bell all wounded her deeply. For much of her adult life she was suicidal, and she finally died by drowning herself in the river Ouse. In "The Death of the Moth" she eloquently describes the death of an insect, a moment that has often served as the foundational experience for mortalism. One thinks—as Woolf herself evidently thought—a) this creature is gone forever, but b) I am just like this creature, so c) when my death comes, it will be just as permanent. As Gerard Manley Hopkins said in a related context, speaking to a child who wept at the sight of dead leaves, "It is the blight man was born for, / It is Margaret you mourn for."

THE DEATH OF THE MOTH

Moths that fly by day are not properly to be called moths; they do not excite that pleasant sense of dark autumn nights and ivy-blossom which the commonest yellow-underwing asleep in the shadow of the curtain never fails to rouse in us. They are hybrid creatures, neither gay like butterflies nor sombre like their own species. Nevertheless the present specimen, with his narrow hay-coloured wings, fringed with a tassel of the same colour, seemed to be content with life. It was a pleasant morning, mid-September, mild, benignant, yet with a keener breath than that of the summer months. The plough was already scoring the field opposite the window, and where the share had been, the earth was pressed flat and gleamed with moisture. Such vigour came rolling in from the fields and the down beyond that it was difficult to keep the eyes strictly turned upon the book. The rooks too were keeping one of their annual festivities; soaring round the tree tops until it looked as if a vast net with thousands of black knots in it had been cast up into the air; which, after a few moments sank slowly down upon the trees until every twig seemed to have a knot at the end of it. Then, suddenly, the net would be thrown down into the air again in a wider circle this time, with the utmost clamour and vociferation, as though to be thrown into the air and settle slowly down upon the tree tops were a tremendously exciting experience.

The same energy which inspired the rooks, the ploughmen, the horses, and even, it seemed, the lean bare-backed downs, sent the moth fluttering from side to side of his square of the window-pane. One could not help watching him. One was, indeed, conscious of a queer feeling of pity for him. The possibilities of pleasure seemed that morning so enormous and so various that to have only a moth's part in life and a day moth's at that, appeared a hard fate, and his zest in enjoying his meager opportunities to the fill, pathetic. He flew vigorously to one corner of his compartment, and, after waiting there a second, flew across to the other. What remained but for him but to fly to a third corner and then to a fourth? That was all he could do, in spite of the size of the downs, the width of the sky, the far-off smoke of houses, and the romantic voice, now and then, of a steamer out at sea. What he could do he did. Watching him, it seemed as if a fibre, very thin but pure, of the enormous energy of the world had been thrust into his frail and diminutive body. As often as he crossed the pane, I could fancy that a thread of vital light became visible. He was little or nothing but life.

Yet, because he was so small, and so simple a form of the energy that was rolling in at the open window and driving its way through so many narrow and intricate corridors in my own brain and in those of other human beings, there was something marvellous as well as pathetic about him. It was as if someone had taken a tiny bead of pure life and decking it as lightly as possible with down and feathers, had set it dancing and zigzagging to show us the true nature of life. Thus displayed one could not get over the strangeness of it. One is apt to forget all about life, seeing it humped and bossed and garnished and cumbered so that it has to move with the greatest circumspection and dignity. Again, the thought of all that life might have been had he been born in any other shape caused one to view his simple activities with a kind of joy.

After a time, tired by his dancing apparently, he settled on the window ledge in the sun, and, the queer spectacle being at an end, I forgot about him. Then, looking up, my eye was caught by him. He was trying to resume his dancing, but seemed either so stiff or so awkward that he could only flutter to the bottom of the window-pane; and when he tried to fly across it he failed. Being intent on other matters I watched these futile attempts for a time without thinking, unconsciously waiting for him to resume his flight, as one waits for a machine, that has stopped momentarily, to start again without considering the reason of its failure. After perhaps a seventh attempt he slipped from the wooden ledge and fell, fluttering his wings, on to his back on the window sill. The helplessness of his attitude roused me. It flashed upon me that he was in difficulties; he could no longer raise himself; his legs struggled vainly. But, as I stretched out a pencil, meaning to help him to right himself, it came over me that the failure and awkwardness were the approach of death. I laid the pencil down again.

The legs agitated themselves once more. I looked as if for the enemy against which he struggled. I looked out of doors. What had happened there? Presumably it was mid-day, and work in the fields had stopped. Stillness and quiet had replaced the previous animation. The birds had taken themselves off to feed in the brooks. The horses stood still. Yet the power was there all the same, massed outside indifferent, impersonal, not attending to anything in particular. Somehow it was opposed to the little hay-coloured moth. It was useless to try to do anything. One could only watch the extraordinary efforts made by those tiny legs against an oncoming doom which could, had it chosen, have submerged an entire city, not merely a city, but masses of human beings; nothing, I knew, had any chance against death. Nevertheless after a pause of exhaustion his legs fluttered again. It was superb, this last protest, and so frantic that he succeeded at last in righting himself. One's sympathies, of course, were all on the side of life. Also, when there was nobody to care or to know, this gigantic effort on the part of an insignificant little moth, against a power of such magnitude, to retain what no one else valued or desired to keep, moved one strangely. Again, somehow, one saw life, a pure bead. I lifted the pencil again, useless though I knew it to be. But even as I did so, the unmistakable tokens of death showed themselves. The body relaxed, and instantly grew stiff. The struggle was over. The insignificant little creature now knew death. As I looked at the dead moth, this minute wayside triumph of so great a force over so mean an antagonist filled me with wonder. Just as life had been strange a few minutes before, so death was now as strange. The moth having righted himself now lay most decently and uncomplainingly composed. O yes, he seemed to say, death is stronger than I am.

(Published in 1942)

JAMES JOYCE (1882-1941)

Unlike Virginia Woolf, his almost exact contemporary, James Joyce was by no means obsessed by death, though he had a healthy fear of it; but death inevitably plays a large role in *Ulysses*, the supreme twentieth-century version of *Everyman*. In the section that follows Leopold Bloom, the unbelieving, deracinated Jewish-Irish hero of Joyce's tale, attends the burial of Paddy Dignam in Dublin's Glasnevin Cemetery as a social courtesy, but he keeps a skeptical and sometimes witty distance from the Catholic pieties surrounding the occasion.

FROM *ULYSSES*

Mr. Kernan said with solemnity:
— *I am the resurrection and the life*. That touches a man's inmost heart.
— It does, Mr. Bloom said.
Your heart perhaps but what price the fellow in the six feet by two with his toes to the daisies? No touching that. Seat of the affections. Broken heart. A pump after all, pumping thousands of gallons of blood every day. One fine day it gets bunged up and there you are. Lots of them lying around here: lungs, hearts, livers. Old rusty pumps: damn the thing else. The resurrection and the life. Once you are dead you are dead. That last day idea. Knocking them all up out of their graves. Come forth, Lazarus! And he came fifth and lost the job. Get up! Then every fellow mousing around for his liver and his lights and the rest of his traps. Find damn all of himself that morning.

* * *

I daresay the soil would be quite fat with corpse manure, bones, flesh, nails, charnelhouses. Dreadful. Turning green and pink, decomposing. Rot quick in damp earth. The lean old ones tougher. Then a kind of tallowy kind of cheesy. Then begin to get black, treacle oozing out of them. Of course the cells or whatever they are go on living. Live for ever practically. Nothing to feed on feed on themselves.

But they must breed a devil of a lot of maggots. Soil must be simply swirling with them. . . . He looks cheerful enough over it. Gives him a sense of power seeing all the others go under first.

Wonder how he looks at life. Cracking his jokes too: warms the cockles of his heart. The one about the bulletin. Spurgeon went to heaven 4 A.M. this morning. 11 P.M. (closing time). Not arrived yet. Peter. The dead themselves the men anyhow would like to hear an odd joke or the women to know what's in fashion.

* * *

Now who is that lankylooking galoot over there in the macintosh? . . . Always someone turns up you never dreamt of. A fellow could live on his lonesome all his life. Yes, he could. Still he'd have to get someone to sod him after he died though he could dig his own grave. We all do. Only man buries. No ants too. First thing strikes anybody. Bury the dead. Say Robinson Crusoe was true to life. Well then Friday buried him. Every Friday buries a Thursday if you come to look at it. . . .

Poor Dignam! His last lie on the earth in his box. When you think of them all it does seem a waste of wood. All gnawed through. They could invent a handsome bier with a kind of panel sliding let it down that way. Ay but they might object to being buried out of another fellows. They're so particular. Lay me in my native earth. Bit of clay from the holy land. Only a mother and a deadborn child ever buried in one coffin. I see what it means. I see. To protect him as long as possible even in the earth. The Irishman's home is his coffin. Embalming in catacombs, mummies, the same idea.

* * *

Gentle sweet air blew round the bared heads in a whisper. Whisper. The boy by the gravehead held his wreath with both hands staring quietly in the black open space. Mr Bloom moved behind the portly kindly caretaker. Well cut frockcoat. Weighing them up perhaps to see which will go next. Well it is a long rest. Feel no more. It's the moment you feel. Must be damned unpleasant. Can't believe it at first. Mistake must be someone else. Try the house opposite. Wait, I wanted to be. I haven't yet. Then darkened deathchamber. Light they want. Whisper around you. Would you like to see a priest? Then rambling and wandering. Delirium all you hid all your life. The death struggle. His sleep is not natural. Press his lower eyelid. Watching is his nose pointed is his jaw sinking are the soles of his feet yellow. Pull the pillow away and finish it off on the floor since he's doomed. Devil in that picture as sinner's death showing him a woman. Dying to embrace her in his shirt. Last act of *Lucia. Shall I nevermore behold thee?* Bam! expires.

Gone at least. People talk about you a bit: forget you. Don't forget to pray for him. Remember him in your prayers. Even Parnell. Ivy day [the memorial observance of the day Charles Stewart Parnell died, October 6, 1891—ed.] dying out. Then they follow: dropping into a hole one after the other.

We are praying now for the repose of his soul. Hoping you're well and not in hell. Nice change of air. Out of the fryingpan of life into the fire of purgatory.

Does he ever think of the hole waiting for himself? They say you do when you shiver in the sun. Someone walking over it. Callboy's warning. Near you. Mine over there towards Finglas, the plot I bought. Mamma poor mamma, and little Rudy.

* * *

Mr Bloom walked unheeded along his grove by saddened angels, crosses, broken pillars, family vaults, stone hopes praying with upcast eyes, old Ireland's hearts and hands. More sensible to spend the money on some charity for the living. Pray for the repose of the soul. Does anybody really? Plant him and have done with him. Like down a coalshoot. Then lump them together to save time. All souls' day. Twentyseventh I'll be at his grave. [Bloom's father, Rudolf Virag, a suicide—ed.] Ten shillings for the gardener. He keeps it free of weeds. Old man himself. Bent down double with his sheers clipping. Near death's door. Who passed away. Who departed this life. As if they did it of their own accord. Got the shove, all of them. Who kicked the bucket. More interesting if they told you who they were. So and so, wheelwright. I travelled for cork lino. I paid five shillings in the pound. Or a woman with her saucepan. I cooked good Irish stew. Eulogy in a country churchyard it ought to be that poem of whose is it Wordsworth or Thomas Campbell. Entered into rest the protestants put it. Old Dr Murren's. The great physician called him home. Well it's God's acre for them. Nice country residence. Newly plastered and painted. Ideal spot to have a quiet smoke and read the *Church Times*. Marriage ads they never try to beautify. Rusty wreaths hung on knobs, garlands of bronzefoil. Better value for the money. Still, the flowers are more poetical. The other gets rather tiresome, never withering. Expresses nothing. Immortelles.

* * *

How many! All these here once walked round Dublin. Faithful departed. As you are now so once were we.

Besides how could you remember everybody? Eyes, walk, voice. Well, the voice, yes: gramophone. Have a gramophone in every grave or keep it in the house. After dinner on a Sunday. Put on poor old greatgrandfather Kraahraark! Hellohelloamarawf amawfullyglad kraark awfullygladaseeeeragain hellohello amarawfkopthsth. Remind you of the voice like the photograph reminds you of the face. Otherwise you couldn't remember the face after fifteen years, say. For instance who? For instance some fellow that died when I was in Wisdom Hely's.

* * *

An obese grey rat toddled along the side of the crypt, moving the pebbles. . . .

One of those chaps would make short work of a fellow. Pick the bones clean no matter who it was. Ordinary meat for them. A corpse is meat gone bad. Well and what's cheese? Corpse of milk. I read in that *Voyages in China* that the Chinese say a white man smells like a corpse. Cremation better. Priest dead against it. Deviling for the other firm. Wholesale burners and Dutch oven dealers. Time of the plague. Quicklime fever pits to eat them. Lethal chamber. Ashes to ashes. Or bury at sea. Where is that parsee tower of silence? Eaten by birds. Earth, fire, water. Drowning they say is the pleasantest. See your whole life in a flash. But being brought back to life no. Can't bury in the air however. Out of a flying machine. Wonder does the news go about whenever a fresh one is let down. Underground communication. We learned that from them. Wouldn't be surprised. Regular square feed for them. Flies come before he's well dead. Got wind of Dignam. They wouldn't care about the smell of it. Saltwhite crumbling mush of corpse: smell, taste like raw white turnips.

The gates glimmered in front: still open. Back to the world again. Enough of this place. Brings you a bit nearer every time. Last time I was here was Mrs. Sinico's funeral. Poor papa too. The love that kills. And even scraping up the earth at night with a lantern like that case I read of to get at fresh buried females or even putrefied with running gravesores. Give you the creeps a bit. I will appear to you after death. You will see my ghost after death. My ghost will haunt you after death. There is another world after death named hell. I do not like that other world she wrote. No more do I. Plenty to see and hear and feel yet. Feel live warm beings near you. Let them sleep in their maggoty beds. They are not going to get me this innings. Warm beds: warm fullblooded life.

(1921)

D. H. LAWRENCE (1885–1930)

L awrence, who died at forty-four from tuberculosis, could be described as
both a vitalist, or life-worshiper, and a mortalist. In "The Ship of Death,"
written shortly before he died but not printed until two years later, Lawrence
sings a kind of incantatory hymn to the power of death. The ship here refers to
toylike bronze ships found in Etruscan burial sites and thought of as a means of
ferrying the souls of the dead to the next world. A writer occasionally given to
preachiness, Lawrence seems to be delivering a vehement sermon to both himself and the human race.

THE SHIP OF DEATH

I

Now it is autumn and the falling fruit
and the long journey toward oblivion.

The apples falling like great drops of dew
to bruise themselves and exit from themselves.

And it is time to go, to bid farewell
to one's own self, and find an exit
from the fallen self.

II

Have you built your ship of death, O have you?
O build your ship of death, for you will need it.

The grim frost is at hand, when the apples will fall
thick, almost thundrous, on the hardened earth.

And death is on the air like a smell of ashes!
Ah! can't you smell it?

And in the bruised body, the frightened soul
finds itself shrinking, wincing from the cold
that blows upon it through the orifices.

III

And can a man his own quietus make
with a bare bodkin?

With daggers, bodkins, bullets, man can make
a bruise or break of exit for his life
but is that a quietus, O tell me, is it quietus?

Surely not so! for how could murder, even self-murder
ever a quietus make?

IV

O let us talk of quiet that we know,
that we can know, the deep and lovely quiet
of a strong heart at peace!

How can we this, our own quietus, make?

V

Build then the ship of death, for you must take
the longest journey, to oblivion.

And die the death, the long and painful death
that lies between the old self and the new.

Already our bodies are fallen, bruised, badly bruised,
already our souls are oozing through the exit
of the cruel bruise.

Already the dark and endless ocean of the end
is washing in through the breaches of our wounds,
already the flood is upon us.

O build your ship of death, your little ark
and finish it with food, with little cakes, and wine
for the dark flight down oblivion.

VI

Piecemeal the body dies, and the timid soul
has her footing washed away, as the dark flood rises.

We are dying, we are dying, we are all of us dying
and nothing will stay the death-flood rising within us
and soon it will rise on the world, on the outside world.

We are dying, we are dying, piecemeal our bodies are dying
and our strength leaves us,
and our soul cowers naked in the dark rain over the flood,
cowering in the last branches of the tree of our life.

VII

We are dying, we are dying, so all we can do
is now to be willing to die, and to build the ship
of death to carry the soul on the longest journey.

A little ship, with oars and food
and little dishes, and all accoutrements
fitting and ready for the departing soul.

Now launch the small ship, now as the body dies
and life departs, launch out, the fragile soul
in the fragile ship of courage, the ark of faith
with its store of food and little cooking pans
and change of clothes,
upon the flood's black waste
upon the waters of the end
upon the sea of death, where we still sail
darkly, for we cannot steer, and have no port.

There is no port, there is nowhere to go
only the deepening blackness darkening still
blacker upon the soundless, ungurgling flood

darkness at one with darkness, up and down
and sideways utterly dark. So there is no direction any more,
and the little ship is there; yet she is gone.
She is not seen, for there is nothing to see her by,
She is gone! gone! and yet
somewhere she is there,
Nowhere!

VIII

And everything is gone, the body is gone
completely under, gone, entirely gone.
The upper darkness is heavy as the lower,
between them the little ship
is gone
she is gone.

It is the end, it is oblivion.

IX

And yet out of eternity, a thread
separates itself on the blackness,
a horizontal thread
that fumes a little with pallor upon the dark.

IS it illusion? or does the pallor fume
a little higher?
Ah wait, wait, for there's the dawn,
the cruel dawn of coming back to life
out of oblivion.

Wait, wait, the little ship
drifting, beneath the deathly ashy grey
of a flood-dawn.

Wait, wait! even so, a flush of yellow
and strangely, O chilled wan soul, a flush of rose.

A flush of rose, and the whole thing starts again.

X

The flood subsides, and the body, like a worn sea-shell
emerges strange and lovely.
And the little ship wings home, faltering and lapsing
on the pink flood,
and the frail soul steps out, into her house again
filling the heart with peace.

Swings the heart renewed with peace
even of oblivion.

Oh build your ship of death, oh build it!
for you will need it,
For the voyage of oblivion awaits you.

(1932)

VLADIMIR NABOKOV
(1899–1977)

In the following brief excerpt from the opening of his autobiography, Nabokov meditates in his usual elegantly saturnine way about the all-engulfing power of death.

FROM *SPEAK, MEMORY*

The cradle rocks above an abyss, and common sense tells us that our existence is but a brief crack of light between two eternities of darkness. Although the two are identical twins, man, as a rule, views the prenatal abyss with more calm than the one he is heading for (at some forty-five hundred heartbeats an hour). I know, however, of a young chronophobiac who experienced something like panic when looking for the first time at homemade movies that had been taken a few weeks before his birth, he saw a world that was practically unchanged—the same house, the same people—and then realized that he did not exist there at all and that nobody mourned his absence. He caught a glimpse of his mother waving from an upstairs window, and that unfamiliar gesture disturbed him, as if it were some mysterious farewell. But what particularly frightened him was the sight of a brand-new baby carriage standing there on the porch, with the smug, encroaching air of a coffin; even that was empty, as if, in the reverse course of events, his very bones had disintegrated.

Such fancies are not foreign to young lives. Or, to put it otherwise, first and last things often tend to have an adolescent note—unless, possibly, they are directed by some venerable and rigid religion. Nature expects a full-grown man to accept the two black voids, fore and aft, as stolidly as he accepts the extraordinary visions in between. Imagination, the supreme delight of the immortal and the immature, should be limited. In order to enjoy life, we should not enjoy it too much.

(1966)

SAMUEL BECKETT (1903–1989)

S amuel Beckett is another modern writer whose every page is tinged with mortalism. In his greatest play *Waiting for Godot* (1950) he provides a variation on Macbeth's characterization of life as a "tale / Told by an idiot, full of sound and fury, / Signifying nothing." The idiot in this case is the grotesquely misnamed Lucky, a deranged slave whose seemingly incoherent babblings are in fact a quite comprehensible but hopeless cry of despair at the absence of God (despite the confident declarations of philosophers and theologians) and the consequent triumph of death ("in spite of the strides of alimentation and defecation"—Lucky's sardonic formula for futile physical existence).

FROM *WAITING FOR GODOT*

Lucky: Given the existence as uttered forth in the public works of Puncher and
Wattmann of a personal God quaquaquaqua outside time without extension who from the heights of divine apathia divine athambia* divine aphasia loves us dearly with some exceptions for reasons unknown but time will tell and suffers like the divine Miranda with those who for reasons unknown but time will tell are plunged in torment plunged in fire whose fire flames if that continues and who can doubt it will fire the firmament that is to say blast hell to heaven so blue still and calm so calm with a calm which even though intermittent is better than nothing but not so fast and considering what is more that as a result of the labors left unfinished crowned by the Acacacacademy of Essy-in-Possy of Testew and Cunard it is established beyond all doubt all other doubt than that which clings to the labors of men that as a result of the labors unfinished of Testew and Cunard it is established as hereinafter but not so fast for reasons unknown that as a result of the public works of Puncher and Wattmann it is established beyond all doubt that in view of the labors of Fartov and Belcher that unfinished for reasons unknown of Testew and Cunard left unfinished it is established what many deny that man in

---

*The inability to wonder.

178

Possy of Testew and Cunard that man in Essy that man in short that man in brief in spite of the strides of alimentation and defectation wastes and pines wastes and pines and concurrently simultaneously what is more for reasons unknown in spite of the strides of physical culture the practice of sports such as tennis football running cycling swimming flying floating riding gliding conating camogie skating tennis of all kinds dying flying sports of all sorts autumn summer winter winter tennis of all kinds hockey of all sorts penicillines and succedanea in a word I resume flying gliding golf over nine and eighteen holes tennis of all sorts in a word for reaons unknown in Feckham Peckham Fulham Clapham namely concurrently simultaneously what is more for reasons unknown but time will tell fades away I resume Fulham Clapham in a word the dead loss per head since the death of Bishop Berkeley being to the tune of one inch four ounce per head approximately by and large more or less to the nearest decimal good measure round figures stark naked to the stockinged feet in Connemara in a word for reasons unknown no matter what matter the facts are there and considering what is more much more grave that in the light of the labors lost of Steinweg and Peterman it appears what is more much more grave that in the light the light the light of the labors lost of Steinweg and Peterman that in the plains in the mountain by the seas by the rivers running water running fire the air is the same and then the earth namely the air and then the earth in the great cold the great dark the air and the earth abode of stones in the great cold alas alas in the year of their Lord six hundred and something the air the earth the sea the earth abode stones in the great deeps the great cold on sea on land and in the air I resume for reasons unknown in spite of the tennis the facts are there but time will tell I resume alas alas on on in short in fine on on abode of stones who can doubt it I resume but not so fast I resume the skull fading fading fading and concurrently simultaneously what is more for reasons unknown in spite of the tennis on on the beard the flames the tears the stones so blue so calm alas alas on on the skull the skull the skull the skull in Connemara in spite of the tennis the labors abandoned left unfinished graver still abode of stones in a word I resume alas alas abandoned unfinished the skull the skull on Connemara in spite of the tennis the skull alas the stones Cunard (*mêlée, final vociferation*) tennis . . . the stones . . . so calm . . . Cunard . . . unfinished . . .

PHILIP LARKIN (1922–1985)

L arkin was a librarian, a novelist, a jazz critic, and a highly original poet. His combination of blunt honesty and self-effacing craftsmaship help to make him one of the great twentieth-century voices of mortalism. Larkin ruefully scans the godless, desolate landscape of his time, but without the nostalgia and anger-at-an-absent-deity of the existentialists.

NEXT, PLEASE

Always too eager for the future, we
Pick up bad habits of expectancy.
Something is always approaching, every day
Till then we say,

Watching from a bluff the tiny, clear,
Sparkling armada of promises draw near.
How slow they are! And how much time they waste,
Refusing to make haste!

Yet still they leave us holding wretched stalks
Of disappointment, for, though nothing balks
Each big approach, leaning with brasswork prinked,
Each rope distinct,

Flagged, and the figurehead with golden tits
Arching our way, it never anchors: it's
No sooner present than it turns to past,
Right to the last

We think each one will heave to and unload
All good into our lives, all we are owed
For waiting so devoutly and so long.
But we are wrong.

Only one ship is seeking us, a black-
Sailed unfamiliar, towing at her back
A huge and birdless silence. In her wake
No waters breed or break.

(1951)

CHURCH GOING

Once I am sure there's nothing going on
I step inside, letting the door thud shut.
Another church: matting, seats, and stone,
And little books; sprawlings of flowers, cut
For Sunday, brownish now; some brass and stuff
Up at the holy end; the small neat organ;
And a tense, musty, unignorable silence,
Brewed God knows how long. Hatless, I take off
My cycle-clips in awkward reverence,

Move forward, run my hand around the font,
From where I stand, the roof looks almost new—
Cleaned, or restored? Someone would know: I don't
Mounting the lectern, I peruse a few
Hectoring large-scale verses, and pronounce
"Here endeth" much more loudly than I'd meant.
The echoes snigger briefly. Back at the door
I sign the book, donate an Irish sixpence,
Reflect the place was not worth stopping for.

Yet stop I did; in fact I often do,
And always end much at a loss like this,
Wondering what to look for; wondering too
When churches fall completely out of use
What we shall turn them into, if we shall keep
A few cathedrals chronically on show,
Their parchment, plate and pyx in locked cases,
And let tbe rest rent-free to rain and sheep.
Shall we avoid them as unlucky places?

Or, after dark, will dubious women come
To make their children touch a particular stone;

Pick simples for a cancer; or on some
Advised night see walking a dead one?
Power of some sort or other will go on
In games, in riddles, seemingly at random;
But superstition, like belief, must die,
And what remains when disbelief has gone?
Grass, weedy pavement, brambles, buttress, sky,

A shape less recognisable each week,
A purpose more obscure. I wonder who
Will be the last, the very last to seek
This place for what it was; one of the crew
That tap and jot and know what rood-lofts were?
Some ruin-bibber, randy for antique,
Or Christmas-addict, counting on a whiff
Of gown-and-bands and organ-pipes and myrrh?
Or will he be my representative,

Bored, uninformed, knowing the ghostly silt
Dispersed, yet tending to this cross of ground
Through suburb scrub because it held unspilt
So long and equably what since is found
Only in separation—marriage, and birth,
And death, and thoughts of those—for which was built
This special shell? For though I've no idea
What this accoutred frowsty barn is worth,
It pleases me to stand in silence here.

A serious house on serious earth it is,
In whose blent air all our compulsions meet,
Are recognized, and robed as destinies.
And that much never can be obsolete,
Since someone will forever be surprising
A hunger in himself to be more serious,
And gravitating with it to this ground,
Which, he once heard, was proper to grow wise in.
If only that so many dead lie round.

(1955)

AMBULANCES

Closed like confessionals, they thread
Loud noons of cities, giving back
None of the glances they absorb.
Light glossy grey, arms on a plaque,
They come to rest at any kerb:
All streets in time are visited.

Then children strewn on steps or road,
Or women coming from the shops
Past smells of different dinners, see
A wild white face that overtops
Red stretcher-blankets momently
As it is carried in and stowed,

And sense the solving emptiness
That lies just under all we do,
And for a second get it whole,
So permanent and blank and true.
The fastened doors recede, *Poor soul*,
They whisper at their own distress;

For borne away in deadened air
May go the sudden shut of loss
Round something nearly at an end,
And what cohered in it across
The years, the unique random blend
Of families and fashion, there
At last begin to loosen. Far
From the exchange of love to lie
Unreachable inside a room
The traffic parts to let go by
Brings closer what is left to come,
And dulls to distance all we are.

(1964)

HEADS IN THE WOMEN'S WARD

On pillow after pillow lies
The wild white hair and staring eyes;
Jaws stand open; necks are stretched
With every tendon sharply sketched;
A bearded mouth talks silently
To someone no one else can see.
Sixty years ago they smiled
At lover, husband, first-born child.
Smiles are for youth. For old age come
Death's terror and delirium.

(1972)

THE OLD FOOLS

What do you think has happened, the old fools,
To make them like this? Do you somehow suppose
It's more grown-up when your mouth hangs open and drools,
And you keep on pissing yourself, and can't remember
Who called this morning? Or that if, if they only chose,
They could alter things back to when they danced all night,
Or went to their wedding, or sloped arms some September?
Or do they fancy there's really been no change,
And they've always behaved as if they were crippled or tight.
Or sat through days of thin continuous dreaming
Watching light move? If they don't (and they can't), it's strange:
        Why aren't they screaming?

At death you break up: the bits that were you
Start speeding away from each other for ever
With no one to see. It's only oblivion, true:
We had it before, but then it was going to end,
And it was all the time merging with a unique endeavour
To bring to bloom the million-petalled flower
Of being here. Next time you can't pretend
There'll be anything else. And these are the first signs:
Not knowing how, not hearing who, the power
Of choosing gone. Their looks show that they're for it:
Ash hair, toad hands, prune face dried into line—
        How can they ignore it?

Perhaps being old is having lighted rooms
Inside your head, and people in them acting.
People you know, yet can't quite name; each looms
Like a deep loss restored, from known doors turning,
Setting down a lamp, smiling from a stair, extracting
A known book from the shelves; or sometimes only
The rooms themselves, chairs and a fire burning,
The blown bush at the window, or the sun's
Faint friendliness on the wall some lonely
Rain-ceased midsummer evening. That is where they live:
Not here and now, but where all happened once.
                              This is why they give

An air of baffled absence, trying to be there
Yet being here. For the rooms grow farther, leaving
Incompetent cold, the constant wear and tear
Of taken breath, and them crouching below
Extinction's alp, the old fools, never perceiving
How near it is. This must be what keeps them quiet;
The peak that stays in view wherever we go
For them is rising ground. Can they never tell
What is dragging them back, and how it will end? Not at night?
Not when the strangers come? Never, throughout
The whole hideous inverted childhood? Well,
                              We shall find out.

                                                        (1973)

AUBADE

I work all day, and get half-drunk at night.
Waking at four to soundless dark, I stare.
In time the curtain-edges will grow light.
Till then I see what's really always there:
Unresting death, a whole day nearer now,
Making all thought impossible but how
And where and when I shall myself die.
Arid interrogation: yet the dread
Of dying, and being dead,
Flashes afresh to hold and terrify.

The mind blanks at the glare. Not in remorse
—The good not done, the love not given, time
Torn off unused—nor wretchedly because
An only life can take so long to climb
Clear of its wrong beginnings, and may never;
But at the total emptiness for ever,
The sure extinction that we travel to
And shall be lost in always. Not to be here,
Not to be anywhere,
And soon; nothing more terrible, nothing more true.

This is a special way of being afraid
No trick dispels. Religion used to try,
That vast moth-eaten musical brocade
Created to pretend we never die,
And specious stuff that says, *No rational being*
Can fear a thing it will not feel, not seeing
That this is what we fear—no sight, no sound,
No touch or taste or smell, nothing to think with,
Nothing to love or link with,
The anaesthetic from which none come round.

And so it stays just on the edge of vision,
A small unfocused blur, a standing chill
That slows each impulse down to indecision.
Most things will never happen: this one will,
And realisation of it rages out
In furnace-fear when we are caught without
People or drink. Courage is no good:
It means not scaring others. Being brave
Lets no one off the grave.
Death is no different whined at than withstood.
Slowly light strengthens, and the room takes shape.
It stands plain as a wardrobe, what we known,
Have always known, known that we can't escape,
Yet can't accept. One side will have to go,
Meanwhile telephones crouch, getting ready to ring
In locked-up offices, and all the uncaring
Intricate rented world begins to rouse.
The sky is white as clay, with no suns,
Work has to be done.
Postmen like doctors go from house to house.

(1977)

L.E. SISSMAN (1928-1976)

Louis Edward Sissman, who worked at all sorts of jobs in publishing, sales, and advertising, died in his late forties from Hodgkin's disease; and out of that grim but slow-moving twist of fate he constructed his haunting poem *Dying: An Introduction*, where he sardonically surveys the leading modern mortalist landscape: hospitals, medical technology, and "quality care." For more on this subject readers should consult Sherwin Nuland's *How We Die*.

DYING: AN INTRODUCTION

Always too eager for the future, we
Pick up bad habits of expectancy.

—Philip Larkin

I. RING AND WALK IN

Summer still plays across the street,
An ad-hoc band
In red, white, blue, and green
Old uniforms
And rented instruments;
Fall fills the street
From shore to shore with leaves,
A jaundiced mass
Protest against the cold;
I slip on ice
Slicks under powder snow and stamp my feet
Upon the doctor's rubber mat,
Ring and Walk in
To Dr. Sharon's waiting room—
For once, with an appointment,
To nonplus

187

Ugly Miss Erberus.
Across from other candidates—
A blue rinsed dam
In Davidows, a husk
Of an old man,
A one-eyed boy—I sit
And share their pervigilium.
One *Punch* and two
Times later comes the call.

II. PROBABLY NOTHING

Head cocked like Art, the *Crimson* linotype
Operator, Dr. Sharon plays
Taps on my game leg, spelling out the name,
With his palpating fingers, of my pain.
The letters he types are not visible
To him or me; back up the melting pot
Of the machine, the matrix dents the hot
Lead with a letter and another; soon a word,
Tinkling and cooling, silver, will descend
To be imposed upon my record in
Black-looking ink. "My boy, I think," he says
In the most masterly of schoolish ways,
In the most quiet of all trumps in A
Flat, "this lump is probably nothing, but"—
A but, a buzz of omen resonates—
"I'd check it anyway. Let's see when I
Can take a specimen." Quiet business
With the black phone's bright buttons. Ssst, ssst, st:
An inside call. In whispers. Over. Out.
"Can you come Friday noon? We'll do it then."
I nod I can, and pass the world of men
In waiting, one *Life* further on.

III. O.P.O.R.*

Undressing in the locker room
Like any high school's, full of shades
In jockstraps and the smell of steam,

---

*Out-Patient Operating Room

Which comes, I guess, from autoclaves,
And not from showers, I am struck
By the immutability,
The long, unchanging, childish look
Of my pale legs propped under me,
Which, nonetheless, now harbor my
Nemesis, or, conceivably,
Do not. My narcissistic eye
Is intercepted deftly by
A square nurse in a gas-green gown
And aqua mask—a dodo's beak—
Who hands me a suit to put on
In matching green, and for my feet
Two paper slippers, mantis green:
My invitation to the dance.
I shuffle to the table, where
A shining bank of instruments—
Service for twelve—awaits my flesh
To dine. Two nurses pull my pants
Down and start shaving. With a splash,
The Doctor stops his scrubbing-up
And walks in with a quiet "Hi."
Like hummingbirds, syringes tap
The Novocain and sting my thigh
To sleep, and the swordplay begins.
The stainless-modern knife digs in—
Meticulous trencherman—and twangs
A tendon faintly. Coward, I groan.
Soon he says, "Sutures," and explains
To me he has his specimen
And will stitch up, with boundless pains,
Each severed layer, till again
He surfaces and sews with steel
Wire. "Stainless." Look how thin it is,
Held in his forceps. "It should heal
Without a mark." These verities
Escort me to the tiring room,
Where, as I dress, the Doctor says,
"We'll have an answer Monday noon."
I leave to live out my three days,
Reprieved from findings and their pain.

IV. PATH. REPORT

Bruisingly cradled in a Harvard chair
Whose orange arms cramp my pink ones, and whose black
Back stamps my back with splat marks, I receive
The brunt of the pathology report,
Bitingly couched in critical terms of my
Tissue of fabrications, which is bad.
That Tyrian specimen on the limelit stage
Surveyed by Dr. Cyclops, magnified
Countless diameters on its thick side,
Turns out to end in -oma. "But be glad
These things are treatable today," I'm told.
"Why, fifteen years ago—" a dark and grave-
Shaped pause. "But now, a course of radiation, and—"
Sun rays break through. "And if you want X-ray,
You've come to the right place." A history,
A half-life of the hospital. Marie
Curie must have endowed it. Cyclotrons,
Like missile silos, lurk within its walls.
It's reassuring, anyway. But bland
And middle-classic as these environs are,
And sanguine as his measured words may be,
And soft his handshake, the webbed, inky hand
Locked on the sill, and the unshaven face
Biding outside the window sill appall
Me as I leave the assignation place.

V. OUTBOUND

Outside, although November by the clock,
Has a thick smell of spring,
And everything—
The low clouds lit
Fluorescent green by city lights;
The molten, hissing stream
Of white car lights cooling
to red and vanishing;
The leaves,
Still running from last summer, chattering,
Across the pocked concrete;
The wind in trees;
The ones and twos,

The twos and threes
Of college girls,
Each shining in the dark,
Each carrying
A book or books,
Each laughing to her friend
At such a night in fall;
The two-and-twos
Of boys and girls who lean
Together in an A and softly walk
Slowly from lamp to lamp,
Alternatively lit
And nighted; Autumn Street,
Astonishingly named, a rivulet
Of asphalt twisting up and back
To some spring out of sight—and everything
recalls one fall
Twenty-one years ago, when I,
A freshman, opening
A green door just across the river,
Found the source
Of spring in that warm night,
Surprised the force
That sent me on my way
And set me down
Today. Tonight. Through my
Invisible new veil
Of finity, I see
November's world—
Low scud, slick street, three giggling girls—
As, oddly, not as sombre
As December,
But as green
As anything: As spring.

(1968)

A DEATHPLACE

Very few people know where they will die,
But I do: in a brick-faced hospital,
Divided, not unlike Caesarean Gaul,
Into three parts: the Dean Memorial
Wing, in the classic cast of 1910,

Green-gated in unglazed Aeolian
Embrasures; the Maud Wiggin Building, which
Commemorates a dog-jawed Boston bitch
Who fought the brass down to their whipcord knees
In World War I, and won enlisted men
Some decent hospitals, and, being rich,
Donated her own granite monument;
The Mandeville Pavilion, pink-brick tent
With marble piping, flying snapping flags
Above the entry where our bloody rags
Are rolled in to be sponged and sewn again.
Today is fair; tomorrow, scourging rain
(If only my own tears) will see me in
Those jaundiced and distempered corridors
Off which the five-foot-wide doors slowly close.
White as my skimpy chiton,* I will cringe
Before the pinpoint of the least syringe;
Before the buttered catheter goes in;
Before the I.V.s lisp and drip begins
Inside my skin; before the rubber hand
Upon the lancet takes aim and descends
To lay me open, and upon its thumb
Retracts the trouble, a malignant plum;
And finally, I'll quail before the hour
When the authorities shut off the power
In that vast hospital, and in my bed
I'll feel my blood go thin, go white, the red,
The rose all leached away, and I'll go dead.
Then will the business of life resume:
The muffled trolley wheeled into my room,
The off-white blanket blanking off my face,
The stealing, secret, private, *largo* race
Down halls and elevators to the place
I'll be consigned to for transshipment, cased
In artificial air and light; the ward
That's underground; the terminal; the morgue.
The one fine day when all the smart flags flap,
A booted man in black with a peaked cap
Will call for me and troll me down the hall
And slot me into his black car. That's all.

(1969)

---

*hospital gown

RICHARD SELZER (1938–)

Selzer is a surgeon, a professor of surgery, and a vivid, sometimes flamboyant writer (see his *Confessions of a Knife* and *Mortal Lessons*). One often has the sense that, like Dickens' Fat Boy, he "wants to make your flesh creep"; and he frequently succeeds. In *Down from Troy* (1992), his autobiography, he traces his medical vocation back to his father, who died when Selzer was only twelve; and who is obviously a major presence in the latter part of the following excerpt, where the second Dr. Selzer returns to a pivotal childhood scene.

DOWN FROM TROY, CHAPTER 12

For each man and woman there is that building of childhood, the mere thought of which years later is enough to reawaken the whole of the buried past. For me it is the Gardner Earl Crematorium. Begun in 1887 and opened for use in 1902, the crematorium stands on a ridge overlooking the city of Troy. I first saw it in the company of Father. The year was 1936. Soon smoke from other crematoria would be drifting across Europe. But we could not know that. We had just left St. Mary's Hospital and, instead of turning toward home, Father pointed the old blue Hudson automobile north on Oakwood Avenue. It was October and we would, he proposed, go see the foliage.

"The Oakwood Cemetery is the best place for leaves," he said. "What with all those maples and oaks, the gravestones will be strewn with them." It is from father that I inherited what mother called my "morbid strain." Just before the entrance to the cemetery and set back from the road was a stone building with a high tower at one end and a tall chimney at the other. The exterior of the building was of rough-hewn gray granite. The silhouette of the rook was broken by pinnacles and turrets. No garden surrounded it; no fountains splashed; no trees stirred. Only a single ancient oak, a Cerberus of a tree, full of gnarled vigor, that brooked no companions. Such a building is a shadow on a child's mind.

"What's the place?" I wanted to know. It could not have been built. It had to have fallen to earth with a terrible thud and squatted there ever since.

Father explained.

"It's the crematorium where people who don't want to buried are burned up in an oven. That"—he pointed—"is the chimney."

"Burned up? That's got to hurt?"

"No it doesn't, silly boy. The dead don't feel pain. They are numb." He had a way of making a word like *numb* reverberate in your ear.

"But how do you know it doesn't hurt?"

"It just doesn't make sense, that's all."

"But you can't prove it, can you?"

With a weary sigh: "No, I can't prove it, as I have never actually been dead. Only half, and that doesn't count."

"Just because we can't hear them hollering . . ."

"We'll go have a look at the leaves," said Father. I could tell that this outing had become his Delilah; already he regretted having lifted the corner of her tent. And well he might, if Mother ever found out where he had taken me, as concerned as she was about my dark cast of mind. But he would not be deterred.

"What happens to the smoke?"

"What do you mean what happens to the smoke? It goes up in the air."

"We breathe it in," I announced grimly.

"It's just particles of soot. After a while, it settles to the ground. Let's look at the leaves."

"It comes down on our food and we eat it."

"The foliage," said Father, "now! And if I were you, I wouldn't mention any of this to your mother. Let it be our secret, yours and mine." Silence. "She is enough worried about you as it is." Silence. "Did you hear me?" "Do you want to smack you with the hairbrush?" I broke the silence.

"You needn't worry, father. I wouldn't dream of telling where you took me." There's nothing worse than a lofty child. At the cemetery we crunched through banks of autumn leaves. How they encrusted the gravestones, red and gold against the white marble.

"Where've you been?" said Billy, affecting indifference. He was as jealous as a cat.

"The crematorium," I replied. The word had been lying on the floor of my mouth. I gathered it up and hummed it at him.

"Crematorium?" said Billy. "What's that?" I told him. "Judas Priest!" he said. The next day after school we walked up to see it.

"It looks like a dragon," said Billy. And so it did! What with its low squat body, the high tower topped by a narrow head, and that rigid tail of a chimney. Even as he spoke, I imagined its horrid feasting, the belching of smoke. All afternoon Billy and I prowled around the building, waiting for something to happen, a revelation that would split open the barriers to the supernatural. There was no sign of life, either inside or out. Still, we had the feeling that we were being watched. It was the dragon itself keeping us in view. All the windows except the two nearest the chimney were of stained glass. You couldn't see through them. Ever since, I have thought the real purpose of stained glass is not decoration but to keep you from seeing what's on the other side. Through the clear windows at the back, by jumping up and down, we could just make out the corner of a pale-green metal box with a row of rivets along the edge.

"The oven!" we exclaimed with a blend of dread and ecstasy. Hours passed while Billy and I scared ourselves to death with eerie moans and shrieks of demonic laughter, casting over-the-shoulder glances to see if the dragon had lashed its tail. Not Thomas Gray and forty country churchyards could have elicited so many shivers. Only missing was the moping owl.

It was the unbreakable rule at our house that children must not be late for meals. Supper was served promptly at six o'clock, You came late to the table, and you went without. But, unbeknownst to us, night had fallen. A mass of dark clouds had muscled across the Hudson Valley. You couldn't see the sky. All at once, the clouds parted to reveal the tower of the crematorium blowing a slender upraised bugle of moon. At that that precise moment a sharp blare of thunder sounded overhead. We jumped right out of the United States. Just as swiftly, the clouds closed. Had we seen the dragon reach up and tear that moon from the sky, we could not have been rendered more lunatic.

Fate, take over! I thought. And so she did. A dark figure stepped from behind the oak tree where it had been lurking, its hideous intention, I knew, bent upon us. In a moment we would be seized by the evil caretaker of the place and flung into his oven. But it was no such thing. It was Father, coming toward us in his long overcoat and his fedora. The sight of the glowing tip of his Lucky Strike was Balm in Gilead. Dizzy with relief, I ran toward him, only to stop just out of arm's reach at a glimpse of his countenance. With a jolt of terrestrial fear, I realized that we had missed supper. It would not go well with us. Holding each of us by an ear, Father marched to the car and tossed us into the backseat.

"We lost track of the time," said Billy. A craven speech that was greeted with the wordless contempt it so richly deserved. The rest of the ride home was made in silence. No sooner were we inside the door than Father pointed his marching finger upstairs to the room Billy and I shared and where all our anguished paraphernalia had flung itself about in sympathy. From the mantel Father took down the silver-plated hairbrush. Nor spake he a single word. None was needed. The firmness with which he closed his grip around the handle was eloquence enough. What a hypocritical thing is a hairbrush that puts itself forward as an article for grooming but is, in fact, a bastinado. *Potch! Potch! Potch! Potch!* When the storm had passed, the netherlands of Troy were on fire. Never mind. It was worth it. For now, Billy and I had in our hearts the very architecture of death. In the months to come, there and there alone would dwell imagination. It would dream of nothing else. Besides we had paid dearly for that crematorium. What comes dearly is dearly held.

Weeks later, pedaling up Oakwood Avenue alone, I saw a row of cars pull up in front of the crematorium.

The first in line was a hearse, I raced to catch up, threw down my bike and ran to hide behind the guardian oak. A small knot of mourners followed the coffin into the building. When I heard the door click shut, I tiptoed to the window, through which I could see the corner of the oven. Minutes went by. The air trembled with premonition. Looking up, I saw issuing from the chimney a thin strand of grayish smoke. It turned slowly in the air like a shroud unwinding, a shroud that kept for a long moment the shape of the human being it had lately enfolded before fanning out over the ridge. That same year I had been reading Dickens— about boys my age who crawled into chimneys to scrape away the soot. Breathed there a sweep so brave as to clean this one? I could not imagine it.

At the turn of the century the population of Troy was almost entirely Irish Catholic. In that faith, cremation was widely held to be repugnant, if not barbarian. It was also an impediment to the resurrection of the flesh. Had there been Jews or Muslims, they would have felt the same way. Most of the crematorium's clients were Protestants from out of town. Any day of the week but Sunday, one of them might arrive on the morning train from New York City. In each party, an extra ticket had been purchased for the body, which was transported as freight. The Union Depot was on Sixth Avenue, one block from where I lived. How often I have imagined it:

Four black-suited men in top hats lower the coffin from a freight car and load it onto a black horse-drawn hearse that is draped in each corner with purples. The heads of the horses are topped with black ostrich plumes; their bellies are tied about with sashes of crepe. Torches blaze from the silver fixtures at the sides of the carriage. There is the muffled solemnity of drums. Other carriages wait for those mourners who cannot manage the steep climb to the cemetery. The rest trail after on foot. The horses turn toward Hoosick Street, stepping slowly, not trotting but in mournful cadence. All along the route, some two miles, citizens halt as the cortege passes by. No man but removes his cap; no woman but crosses herself and moves her lips in whispers for the repose of the defunct.

Time and again during the fifty years that have passed, I have dispatched my dreaming mind to that ridge overlooking the Hudson River, to that building whose spell, cast over me in childhood has never been lifted. At last the day has come when I have left the armchair on the little study in New Haven where I read and write, and I have returned to Troy to confront the crematorium.

I'm standing at the gates to the Oakwood Crematorium. To my left the crematorium is comprised of equal parts of light and shadow. I see that the oak tree is no more. Nor is there any sign of a stump. When had it wrenched up its arthritic roots and limped off? Instead, there is a lawn civilized with precisely clipped evergreen shrubs. It is noon, but not even the noonday sun reveals this place. Rather, it is the visitor who is revealed to the building. It knows my fate. Standing before it, I am aware of the sixty years, my gray hair, "the wormy circumstance" of my clothes. Here is a building that has the appearance of having been built yesterday. A hundred years of rain and wind have made no mark upon it. It is as it was at the beginning, a building that had no infancy, had no ripening to do, but was from the moment of its construction fully adult. It is impossible not to think of an animal, a frozen mammoth in Siberia or a creature that has crawled up from deep beneath the ground and that sleeps and sleeps until, stirred by hunger, it awakens with a fire in its belly.

Arrangements have been made and I am to be guided by a caretaker, who is walking toward me, keys in hand. A more unlikely Charon could not be imagined. Tom Gibson is thirty-one, short, pigeon plump, with a blond beard, Irish good looks and a welcoming smile. He wears a baseball cap and a jacket with the words NEW YORK GIANTS on the back. In his running shoes he is a muscular, soft-footed cat. Together we walk the perimeter of the crematorium. The building faces the east, from which it receives the first rays of the rising sun. It is one hundred and forty-six feet in length and, at its widest, seventy-five. The chapel and its tower are connected by loggia comprised of three massive arches. From the northernmost roof rises the tall slender chimney, flared gracefully at the top. The square tower is eighteen feet around and ninety feet high. Seventy feet up is a balcony. Above this is the belfry, which is open on all four sides. Between the tower and the chimney lies a profusion of turrets, pinnacles, and gables. No longer of slate, the roof is now of molded copper. The impression is not at all that of a church. It is, instead, a sarcophagus, which, as the ancient Greeks believed, ate the flesh placed within it, leaving behind the indigestible bones. The walls, tower and chimney, all in gray granite, suggest secrecy, as though a gray cloak has been thrown over the interior. Overlooking the Hudson River Valley, the crematorium suggests the patience of the immortal that waits for the inconsequential to get itself over with.

At the rear of the building, a tame garage lies tethered. Through its open door, I see a backhoe, a squadron of lawnmowers, tree saws, picks and shovels. The caretaker explains that he and his two helpers must, in addition to their crematorium duties, mow the grass in the cemetery, prune dead branches, dig the graves, lower the coffins, replace the earth, set the stones.

"That's a lot of work," I tell him.

"Yeah? You think so? Well, there ain't any hurry, What don't get done, waits." Together the caretaker and I mount the steps to the loggia. Passing beneath an arch changes one so. On the other side is always an altogether different domain entered with trepidation and expectancy. Anything might happen there. Tom Gibson unlocks the door to the tower at the southern end of the loggia. He leads the way as we climb a marble-and-wrought-iron spiral staircase to a landing. A second spiral staircase brings us to the base of an iron ladder, which we ascend hand over hand to the belfry. There is no longer a bell. In its place, swarming from a hive in the eaves, a thousand bees offer their bronze hum so that the air vibrates as after a gong has been struck. The caretaker, wary of them, pulls at his cap. If the chimney is the tail of the beast, this belfry is its eye. Far below us stretches the whole of the valley. I see the confluence of the Mohawk and the Hudson Rivers, the Cohoes Falls, the towns that line either bank—Cohoes, Watervliet, and Troy itself. At our feet, the copper sheets of the roof gleam. Yes! like the scales of a dragon.

When I have seen enough, Tom leads the way down and unlocks the door of the chapel. Here he stands aside to let me enter. With that first glance, I have the sense that I have seen this room before. But where? In a former life, perhaps. Or had it until now remained, like Psyche's grotto, an untrodden chamber of my mind? Immediately upon crossing the threshold, I am not in a building at all but aboard a yacht whose wardrooms and cabins are fitted out with every sumptuous furnishing, each meant to divert the passenger's attention from the pitching seas all around. The ceiling of the chapel is of quartered oak with intricate open timberwork. The chairs and benches are of the same wood. The floor is of bluestone. There are four large Tiffany stained-glass windows—ruby and dark blue with greenish lights. The walls and all the fixtures are of red-and-black marble.

The reception room is even more clamorous, with pillars of green onyx, blind arcades, bronze doors and walls of pink-and-gray marble. No use to listen for a still, small voice above this din. Try as they might, these furnishings do not deceive. Each bit of decor by itself is beautiful. Taken together they give off a faint, sickish vulgarity. It is a place you inhabit in a claustrophobic nightmare from which you awake terrified and gasping. All the powers of sensory persuasion cannot distract the thoughts from the box full of fire.

It is evening. I have said goodnight to the caretaker and we have arranged to meet tomorrow at noon. Perhaps I should not have come here in March, when the light is pale and troubled. March is what is left of winter; it is winter hanging by a thread.

It is the next day, and I am to witness a cremation. At precisely three-thirty, a hearse arrives and backs up to the entrance of the retort room. In the hearse are three long flat cardboard boxes, each one labeled. The word HEAD is printed at one end of each box. Tom and his helpers, Rich and Lou, slide the boxes onto waist-high carts fitted out with rollers. Papers of identification and receipt are checked and signed. The hearse departs. Tom presses the button that raises the doors of the ovens. They are lined with firebrick. In each, a trough runs partly down the middle of the floor. The men slide the boxes one by one from the carts, each into its own oven. Buttons are pressed; the doors are lowered.

"I'll show you how it works," says Tom. Watching this caretaker at his valves and buttons, I think again of Father. I see him ceremonially rolling up his shirt sleeves, then kneeling into the fireplace to set the kindling, holding each log gently and with respect in his beautiful priest's hands.

"You have to set one next to the other just so," he would say. "They've got to touch in order for the fire to pass back and forth between them. Be sure to leave room for air so that the first little flame can breathe." He might have been instructing us in the act of love. Moments later—it never failed—a blaze, and his tiny smile of pride and pleasure. At intervals, Mother, with a kerchief over her hair, collected the ashes and sprinkled them on her house plants.

"There's nothing like ashes to make the begonias grow," she'd say.

No one else was permitted to set and light a fire at our house. Once, like Prometheus, I stole a box of kitchen matches and Billy and I set fire to some old crates in the empty lot at the back of the house. It says something about the impoverishment of the modern imagination that while Prometheus's punishment for the same crime was to be chained to a rock and have his liver pecked out by an eagle, Billy and I suffered only the same old hairbrush used for any mundane infraction. Not until I was thirteen and Father had died did I make a fire in the hearth. It was a short-lived, smoky affair that told me point blank that I wasn't ready yet. Ever since, the most cheerful blaze in a fireplace contains for me one ember of that old sorrow. From father I learned that fire ends life, then sets it forth in a new existence. In the heart of the fire, death is no longer death; it has been annulled by the flames. And here, in this crematorium, is the crucible where this transformation is enacted.

"The head and the heart take the longest time to burn up," says Tom. "Arms and legs don't need more than an hour. The hottest place is closer to the door. That's why they got to go in feet first. We give it three hours anyway at fourteen hundred degrees Fahrenheit, just to be sure." He presses the starter buttons and blowers, and sets the automatic shut-off. Rich and Lou get in an old red truck labeled TROY CEMETERY ASSOCIATION and go off for coffee.

"I'll show you where we keep the remains," says Tom. We climb a flight of stairs to a room lined with shelves laden with urns of ashes, bouquets of artificial flowers and photographs of the dead.

"I wouldn't want to be put here," I tell him.

"You wouldn't?"

"No, I'd rather be scattered somewhere." It is the one preference I am sure of.

"We've got bags and bags of ashes in the basement. No one even knows who they are."

Rich and Lou have come back with the coffee. They toot for us to come and get it. The four of us stand around outside drinking and smoking cigarettes. Above, flames are shooting out of the chimney.

"Okay," says Tom. "Now I'll give you a look inside. It's been on for half an hour." He presses the OPEN button. The door rises and a blast of heat slaps my face. The smell of meat roasting seeks out my mouth, fills the back of my throat. There is the sound of spitting and of the flames rolling their R's. Inside, the corpse is animated, the head thrown back so that the face is visible, the mouth darkly agape, lips shrunk to the gums. The bosses of the skull are bright as butter in the firelight. And as yellow. The arms, which had been at the sides, are lifted as if to fend something off. As I watch, there is a slow washing movement of the hands. In the trough below, a liquid bubbling.

"The lady wasn't embalmed," says the caretaker. He points to the trough. "Those are the body fluids."

"How do you know that?" I ask him.

"How do I know what?"

"That it's a . . . a . . . lady?" The word is uneasy in my mouth.

"Oh, I can tell all right. I can tell." At that moment, it might have been Father shaking his head sadly. "So," he would be saying, "you have learned nothing. Fifty years ago you gave back to the dead the curse of sensation. And still you do."

"No, no," I whisper to his shade. "The dead lose all reticence, and speak more freely than the living."

"You!" I hear him give a deep sigh of damnation, "You'll never grow up."

I am aware that the three—Tom, Rich, and Lou—are watching me. There is mischief in their smiles, the way they glance at one another, humor overflowing their eyes. They are boys, playing navy, floating their ships in the pond, then setting them on fire. All three are immensely proud of their work, and lighthearted, peppy as though refreshed by the presence of death. I have none of their sangfroid. Above the voices of the oven, it is Tom's voice that leads me by the hand.

"It's somethin' you don't take personally," he says. The others nod. "It don't bother me none. I even had two of my best buddies in here. Slid 'em right on in, and turned on the gas myself. I was glad I could do it for 'em."

I see that these men have moved beyond the horrific, where I am trapped. It is not that their imaginations have been blunted; it is that mine is overheated. That "morbid" cast of mind. Tom closes the oven door. All that remains of that hellfire lies in my eyes. We shake hands and plan to meet again in the morning. Outside, rain is falling, Troy is filled with its green fragrance.

When I arrive, the ovens have been swept out. A frost of ashes clings to the firebrick, as though not heat but cold had raged there. Rich is carrying a bin of cinders to a stone table. Among them lie fragments of bone an inch or more in length. Here and there I recognize a ridge or a groove where once a muscle arose or inserted. It is Rich's job to pound them into ashes. With each blow of his hammer, a small cloud of dust rises. His hands are white with it. His face, too. When he has finished, he scoops the ashes into an urn and labels it. Then on to the next.

"We do five hundred a year," says Tom. "You got any questions?"

"How much does it cost?" It is all I can think to ask.

"Only one hundred and thirty dollars."

"That *is* cheap."

Tom turns to Rich. "We gonna lift tonight?"

"Yeah."

"Lift?" I say,

Tom explains. "Me and Rich lift weights sometimes after work."

It is the fourth day of my visit. The caretaker has brought me as far as he can. For the remainder of my stay he has lent me a key to the crematorium. I am to come and go as I please. The weather has turned cold. It has snowed, melted, frozen. The north side of the belfry shows fangs of ice. At the hotel, they have lit a fire in the tavern. I sit facing it. Each time I raise my glass, it fills with feathered orange, until what I am drinking is fire.

Day after day I roam the languid undulations of the cemetery hills or go to sit alone in the raftered gallery. With each hour the impulse to scoff at what I had first seen as sentimental clichés of the hereafter grows dimmer. What had seemed a duplicity of furnishings has become a purity of intention. I see it in the reddish marble whose arterial tracery streams with golden corpuscles. I see it in the gules—blood and grape—transmitted through the stained glass as the sun moves across the sky. How they tremble on the walls, the floor, quickening the dark skeleton of oaken ribs, taking the gloom.

They were honest masons who made this place a hundred years ago, they who had hewed and carved, etched and polished, fashioning their version of paradise out of a passion for their trowels and chisels. Perhaps those men had no conception of art; perhaps they were untouched by learning. It doesn't matter. The work of their hands had a holiness of its own, and to those whose sensibilities have not been dulled by excessive intellect or cynicism, the holiness is still there a century later.

It is time to leave the dew-struck hills of Troy and return to the round of my life. In the week since I arrived, I have gazed and gazed. And gazed myself out. The crematorium has spoken, yielding up its secret and instructing me how to live. Or rather, how to die. Minutes ago, I signed a form "solemnly expressing" to my next of kin my wish to be cremated in this building when the time comes. In the place where it called for a witness, Tom Gibson writes his name. He walks me to my car.

"Tom," I say. "What's your idea of the hereafter? Or is it all just a box of ashes so far as you're concerned?"

"The next life?" He smiles, shrugs. "About that I wouldn't want to say." He looks off into the distance. "Sometimes I watch those flames shooting out of the chimney and I wonder."

I go to open a car door. But I don't yet. On the door handle, a butterfly. Come so early. It is black, edged with sulfur. Slowly, the upright wings open and close. I feel the pulse captive in them. The soft valvular systole. Diastole.

(1992)

MARGARET ATWOOD (1939–)

Better known as a novelist (*The Handmaid's Tale*, 1986), Atwood, a Canadian, is also a good poet, as this understated elegy for her father shows.

FLOWERS

Right now I am the flower girl.
I bring fresh flowers,
dump out the old ones, the greenish water
that smells like dirty teeth
into the bathroom sink, snip off the stem ends
with surgical scissors I borrowed
from the nursing station,
put them into a jar
I brought from home, because they don't have vases
in this hotel for the ill.
place them on the table beside my father
where he can't see them
because he won't open his eyes.

He lies flattened under the white sheet.
He says he is on a ship,
and I can see it—
the functional white walls, the minimal windows,
the little bells, the rubbery footsteps of strangers,
the whispering all around
of the air-conditioner, or else the ocean,
and he is on a ship;
he's giving us up, giving up everything
but the breath going in
and out of his diminished body;
minute by minute he's sailing slowly away,

away from us and our waving hands
that do not wave.

The women come in, two of them, in blue;
it's no use being kind, in here,
if you don't have hands like theirs—
large and capable, the hands
of plump muscular angels,
the ones that blow trumpets and lift swords.
They shift him carefully, tuck in the corners.
It hurts, but as little as possible.
Pain is their lore. The rest of us
are helpless amateurs.
A suffering you can neither cure nor enter—
there are worse things, but not many.
After a while it makes us impatient.
Can't we do anything but feel sorry?

I sit there, watching the flowers
in their pickle jar. He is asleep, or not.
I think: he looks like a turtle.
Or: He looks erased.
But somewhere in there, at the far end of the tunnel
of pain and forgetting he's trapped in
is the same father I knew before,
the one who carried the green canoe
over the portage, the painter trailing,
myself with the fishing rods, slipping
on the wet boulders and slapping flies.
That was the last time we went there.

There will be a last time for this also,
bringing cut flowers to this white room.
Sooner or later I too
will have to give everything up,
even the sorrow that comes with these flowers,
even the anger,
even the memory of how I brought them
from a garden I will no longer have by then,
and put them beside my dying father,
hoping I could still save him.

(1995)

JAMES FENTON (1949–)

A journalist, critic, translator, and academic, Fenton shows in his cheerfully irreverent ballad, "God: A Poem" that mortalism doesn't have to be tragic or solemn.

GOD, A POEM

A nasty surprise in a sandwich,
A drawing-pin caught in your sock,
The limpest of handshakes from a hand which
You'd thought would be firm as a rock.

A serious mistake in a nightie,
A grave disappointment all round
Is all that you'll get from th'Almighty,
Is all that you'll get underground.

Oh, he *said*: "If you lay off the crumpet*
I'll see you alright in the end.
Just hang on till the last trumpet.
Have faith in me, chum—I'm your friend."

But if you remind him, he'll tell you:
"I'm sorry, I must have been pissed—
Though your name rings sort of a bell. You
Should have guessed that I do not exist.

"I didn't exist at Creation,
I didn't exist at the Flood,

---

*women

And I won't be around for Salvation
To sort out the sheep from the cud—

"Or whatever the phrase is. The fact is
In soteriological terms
I'm a crude existential malpractice
And you are a diet of worms.

"You're a nasty surprise in a sandwich,
You're a drawing-pin caught in my sock.
You're the limpest of shakes from a hand which
I'd have thought would be firm as a rock.

"You're a serious mistake in a nightie,
You're a grave disappointment all round—
That's all that you are," says th'Almighty,
"And that's all that you'll be underground."

                                                    (1983)

GJERTRUD SCHNACKENBERG
(1953–)

In this richly detailed and allusive poem (note the web of references to Shakespeare's *The Tempest*, at the very end of which Prospero vows to retire to Milan, "where every third thought shall be my grave") about Charles Darwin not long before his death, Schnackenberg evokes a powerful sense of impending and permanent mortality.

DARWIN IN 1881

Sleepless as Prospero back in his bedroom
In Milan, with all his miracles
Reduced to sailors' tales,
He sits up in the dark. The islands loom.
His seasickness upwells,
Silence creeps by in memory as it crept
By him on water, while the sailors slept,
From broken eggs and vacant tortoise shells.
His voyage around the cape of middle age
Comes, with a feat of insight, to a close,
The same way Prospero's
Ended before he left the stage
To be led home across the blue-white sea,
When he had spoken of the clouds and globe,
Breaking his wand, and taking off his robe:
Knowledge increases unreality.

He quickly dresses.
Form wavers like his shadow on the stair
As he descends, in need of air
To cure his dizziness,
Down past the ship-sunk emptiness

206

Of grownup children's rooms and hallways where
The family portraits stare,
All haunted by each other's likenesses.

Outside, the orchard and a piece of moon
Are islands, he an island as he walks,
Brushing against weed stalks.
By hook and plume
The seeds gathering on his trouser legs
Are archipelagoes, like nests he sees
Shadowed in branching, ramifying trees,
Each with unique expressions in its eggs.
Different islands conjure
Different beings, different beings call
From different isles. And after all
His scrutiny of Nature
All he can see
Is how it will grow small, disappear,
A coastline fading from a traveler
Aboard a survey ship. Slowly,
As coasts depart,
Nature had left behind a naturalist
Bound for a place where species don't exist,
Where no emergence has a counterpart.

He's heard from friends
About the other night, the banquet hall
Ringing with bravos—like a curtain call,
He thinks, when the performance ends,
Failing to summon from the wings
An actor who had lost his taste for verse,
Having beheld, in larger theaters,
Much greater banquet vanishings
Without the quaint device and thunderclap
Required in Act 3.
He wrote, Let your indulgence set me free,
To the Academy, and took a nap
Beneath a *London Daily* tent,
Then puttered on his hothouse walk
Watching his orchids beautifully stalk
Their unreturning paths, where each descendant
Is the last—

Their inner staircases
Haunted by vanished insect faces
So tiny, so intolerably vast.
And, while they gave his proxy the award,
He dined in Downe and stayed up rather late
For backgammon with his beloved mate,
Who reads his books and is, quite frankly, bored.

Now, done with beetle jaws and beaks of gulls
And bivalve hinges now, utterly done,
One miracle remains, and only one.
An ocean swell of sickness rushes, pulls,
He leans against the fence
And lights a cigarette and deeply draws,
Done with fixed laws,
Done with experiments
Within his greenhouse heaven where
His offspring, Frank, for half the afternoon
Played, like an awkward angel, his bassoon
Into the humid air
So he could tell
If sound would make a Venus's-flytrap close.
And, done for good with scientific prose,
That raging hell
Of tortured grammars writhing on their stakes,
He'd turned to his memoirs, chuckling to write
About his boyhood in an upright
Home: a boy preferring gartersnakes
To schoolwork, a lazy, strutting liar
Who quite provoked her aggravated look,
Shushed in the drawing room behind her book,
His bossy sister itching with desire
To tattletale—yes, that was good.
But even then, much like the conjurer
Grown cranky with impatience to abjure
All his gigantic works and livelihood
In order to immerse
Himself in tales where he could be the man
In Once upon a time there was a man.

He'd quite by chance beheld the universe:
A disregarded game of chess

Between two love-dazed heirs
Who fiddle with the tiny pairs
Of statues in their hands, while numberless
Abstract unseen
Combinings on the silent board remain
Unplayed forever when they leave the game
To turn, themselves, into a king and queen.
Now, like the coming day,
Inhaled smoke illuminates his nerves.
he turns, taking the sandwalk as it curves
back to the yard, the house, the entrance way
Where, not to waken her,

He softly shuts the door,
And leans upon it for a spell before
He climbs the stairs, holding the banister,
Up to their room: there
Emma sleeps, moored
In illusion, blown past the storm he conjured
With his book, into a harbor
Where it all comes clear,
Where island beings leap from shape to shape
As to escape
Their terrifying turns to disappear.
He lies down on the quilt,
He lies down like a fabulous headed
Fossil in a vanished riverbed,
In ocean drifts, in canyon floors, in silt
In lime, in deepening blue ice,
In cliffs obscured as clouds gather and float;
He lies down in his boots and overcoat,
And shuts his eyes.

(1982)

WILLIAM R. CLARK (1938–)

It seems fitting to end this anthology with remarks by a scientist, since, how-ever instinctive and intuitive the roots of mortalism may be, its ultimate foun-dations rest on empirical observation of the natural world, above all from the growing evidence that so-called spiritual phenomena all derive from, and perish with, our perishable bodies, In *Sex and the Origins of Death*, Clark, a professor of Immunology at University of California at Los Angeles, brilliantly rings the changes on the by-now familiar notion that the only absolutely necessary func-tion humans (along with other living creatures) serve is to pass along their DNA. Having done so (or not) they are ready for permanent personal extinction (being tossed into what Vladimir Nabokov once called "nature's garbage bin"). As Clark shows, not only do our cells die from trauma, infection, wear and tear, etc., but they actually commit suicide in a form of preprogrammed degeneration called apoptosis. The process is undeniably eerie—and eerily undeniable.

SEX AND THE ORIGINS OF DEATH

EPILOGUE

And every time again and again I make my lament against destruction.
—Yevgeny Yevtushenko

We die because our cells die. Clearly the definition of humanness must transcend descriptions that can be derived from studying the lives of individual cells; yet it is true that when death comes for us it gathers us in cell by cell by cell. The death of our cells, as we have seen, is not an a priori requirement of life. It is an evo-lutionary consequence of the way we reproduce ourselves, and of our multicel-lularity. For reasons which are difficult to discern across thousands of millions of years of evolutionary time, the decision to use sex as a means of reproduction was followed, in the evolutionary line reading to human beings, by the genera-tion of reproductively irrelevant DNA. The irrelevant DNA, segregated off into somatic cells, has become us.

DNA has only one goal: to reproduce itself. It does this in accordance with the same physical laws—the same principles of thermodynamics—that govern all the rest of the universe. Once a reasonable number of our germ cells have been given a chance to impart their DNA to the next generation, our somatic cells become so much excess baggage. They serve no useful function, and they—we must die, so that change can be transmitted to the next generation.

Under the guidance of DNA, every somatic cell in the body will senesce and ultimately die on its own. This has come to be known as a programmed death. If the cells escape accidental cell death, they will ultimately be instructed to commit suicide—to execute the sequence of events known as programmed cell death via apoptosis. Most often this happens when the DNA of a cell has accumulated unacceptable levels of DNA damage. But death of a body rarely if ever occurs because of the cumulative effects of sequential, one-by-one extinction of somatic cells. Autopsies of very old people (over eighty years of age) usually reveal signs of a half a dozen or more serious ailments that could have been expected to lead shortly after death. Sooner or later, as cells gradually die off through apoptosis and critical organs such as the kidneys or lungs or liver begin to fail because of cell loss, the heart will stop beating. Then the death process takes place in a greatly accelerated fashion. Deprived of nutrients and oxygen carried by the blood, the remaining cells in the body will die a violent necrotic death in a matter of minutes. Brain cells will be the first to go; the rest will soon follow.

Whether cells die by necrosis or apoptosis, the key element in their demise is the loss of the carefully integrated cellular structure that allows metabolism to sustain itself. In necrotic cell death, structure is disrupted mostly by the influx of water, stretching and tearing and pulling the cell apart. In apoptosis, internal structures (aside from DNA) are not altered so much as segregated from one another as the cell disintegrates into apoptotic bodies. The individual organelles are all there, but they can no longer interact. A collection—even a complete collection—of organelles in separate apoptotic bodies is no more a cell than a collection of busy organs in separate bags is a human being. The individual organ structures are still there, and may function for a while, but the structure of the organism is lost forever. So it is with a cell dying by apoptosis, shedding parts of itself like petals from a flower, or leaves from a tree.

The order in which somatic cells die is of no particular concern to nature, although recently it has become of increasing concern to us. When the heart stops pumping, the brain cells die first, as we have seen. Other cells follow, the timing of their deaths determined by their ability to carry out anaerobic metabolism with food stores set aside for leaner times. No one seems to have kept (or at least published) accurate records on the point, but we could very likely recover viable cells such as fibroblasts from a human being for quite some time after complete loss of brain function and an official declaration of death. Put into culture, these cells could proceed to complete their Hayflick limit [the point at which such cells stop dividing and eventually die—ed.] for many weeks or months after the body from which they came had died, until they finally succumbed to their own genetically encoded deaths by apoptosis. Unless, of course, they somehow got transformed by a virus, in which case they might carry germ DNA hologram endlessly into the future like some renegade germ cell, or like the cells taken from Henrietta Lack's tumor. [Henrietta Lacks, d. 1951, had a particularly virulent form of cancer, sample cells of which, the so-called HeLa cells, have been grown in laboratories around the world and continue to be used in research—ed.].

We have learned to intervene in the death process started by the loss of heart cells, and in some cases this intervention works very well. The formerly rapid and irreversible slide toward death can often be halted. A defective heart can be replaced, either by a transplant, or possibly one day, by a completely artificial heart; the heart, in the end, is simply a pump. Certain types of damage to the brain can be repaired, too, but once neurons die they cannot be brought back to life, and they cannot be replaced. The technology of resuscitation has forced us to face squarely the issue of death as it relates to brain function; we are moving ever closer to the notion that the death of too many cells in the cortex of the brain signals the death of a person, if not of the body. Yet even this redefinition may not be sufficient to address the problems we have created for ourselves. As Peter Singer, the eminent Australian bioethicist, has stated in his book *Rethinking Life and Death*: "The patching [up] could go on and on and on, but it is hard to see a long and beneficial future for an ethic as paradoxical, incoherent and dependent on pretense as our conventional ethic of life and death has become. New medical techniques, decisions in landmark legal cases, and shifts of public opinion are constantly threatening to bring the whole edifice crashing down."

Nevertheless, for the present, human beings seem to have decided that cells of the brain are more important in defining life than other cells. Nature, of course, would make no such distinction; from her point of view, a brain is no more or less important than a lung a kidney or a foot. Nature recognizes no hierocracy among somatic cells. Why do we make such a distinction if nature does not? The brain evolved to coordinate the activities of the body more effectively, to make the organism it directs better at competing for resources, for survival, and for the right to pass on a particular set of genes—a particular pattern of DNA. But somewhere along the way the human brain took a completely unprecedented turn; it acquired a mind. This meant nothing at all to nature, except as it might promote the welfare of DNA, but it took us, as biological organisms, into distinctly nonbiological arenas apparently having little to do with survival and reproduction: poetry, for example, or pure reason or pure mathematics; art, religion, and music; sitcoms and soap operas. The pressures that govern our own further evolution are no longer strictly biological; through mind we have acquired culture, and that, rather than a competition for resources needed to survive until breeding age, is now the dominant selective force in our reproductive success. As Richard

Dawkins has pointed out, although culture exists only in our minds, it neverthe-less has its own evolutionary momentum, just as genes and DNA do.

We have yet to see how or to what extent or even whether the acquisition of mind may have changed or may yet change the natural order of things. Human beings have escaped the harsh realities of natural selection, but the rest of the biological planet has not. It is not simply that we have created mental pastimes which make our passage through life more pleasant, or at least more tolerable; through mind, we have begun to alter nature, and even our biological selves, in ways never before seen in the biosphere in which we evolved. No longer subject to the early and harsh death nature reserves for the weak or the unfit, we have begun to accumulate genetic defects that would long ago have been culled by nature. Medicine in the twentieth century has already enabled us to alter the composition of the human gene pool by keeping alive through reproductive age people who, in a more natural environment, would have died of genetic disease. Medicine in the twenty-first century, through gene therapy, will extend this trend into frontiers still only vaguely perceived, and with genetic consequences that can only be guessed at. And not content to have escaped the competition for resources imposed on other living things, we have begun to alter by pollution and to deplete by consumption those resources upon which other life forms depend. This may not be without a price. Most of us have become aware that depletion of natural resources deprives us of species whose beauty or grace or physical prowess we admire and whose absence from this planet we would mourn. What we are only dimly beginning to perceive is that these species are in turn the nat-ural habitat of a range of microbial organisms with whom they lived for millions of years in peaceful equilibrium. Deprived of their natural hosts some of these micro-organisms, out of sheer desperation, have begum to jump to humans where there is no such equilibrium, and may not be for millions of years to come. The results, as we have seen with Ebola and AIDS viruses, can be disastrous.

Our minds have come to regard our bodies as something more than a fancy vehicle for nurturing and transmitting DNA, and have made us unwilling to let reproduction be, as it is for all other living creatures, our only imperative, our only impact on the world in which we live. We have become thinking creatures that think about a great deal more than DNA. As the story about the brain sur-geon shows, the brain through mind can even think about itself. But the mind contemplating the brain—and thus itself—is a bit like looking into a mirror with another mirror behind your back; it triggers an endless array of front and rear images tapering off into infinity. So when we try to think of the universe and our own place in it, when we think about what defines us as a human, or about life and death, perhaps we should retain certain skepticism about our conclusions. We must remember that whatever notions we may hold about the importance of the brain as mind, those notions originated in the mind as brain. In any other aspect of human affairs, this would be considered a conflict of interest. It is a humbling thought, but the human mind is not the power that drives the universe. Whether we like it or not, the mind as brain is driven ultimately by DNA, this bizarre molecule that is in turn driven—mindlessly, we presume, yet somehow desperately—to reproduce itself.

When we complete the dying process, every single cell in our body will be dead, as nature intended. If we have done our bidding, we will pass on our DNA, packaged in germ cells, to the next generation. That DNA may very well be standing next to our death bed in the form of a son or a daughter. The DNA in all the rest of the cells in our body—our somatic DNA—will no longer be of any use; like the DNA in the first redundant macronucleus a billion or so years ago, it will be destroyed. To paraphrase an old biological saw, a human being is just a germ cell's way of making another germ cell—as is a cockroach, as is a cabbage. This is not a very flattering way to explain ourselves to ourselves. We want so desperately to be more than just a vehicle for DNA, and at least transiently we are. Yet somatic cells will die at the end of each generation, whether they are part of an insect wing or a human brain. We may come to understand death, but we cannot change this single, simple fact: in the larger scheme of things, it matters not a whit that some of these somatic cells contain all that we hold most dear about ourselves; our ability to think, to feel, to love—to write and read these very words. In terms of the basis process of life itself, which is the transmission of DNA from one generation to the next, all of this is just so much sound and fury, signifying certainly very little, and quite possibly nothing.

(1996)

54479

BIBL. UNIV. DE / OF SUDBURY LIBR.

3 0007 00775 4475